David –

Education

employed for th present. Good

press leads good people.

¡ Dale Fuerte!

Mike

The Modern Charity

By
Mike Stewart

One America

From the tip of Canada to tail of Argentina is one large connected body of America. South of the States consists of more than 570 million residents making up 8.5% of the world's population. Yet America must become reacquainted with America. A desire to involve itself in the process of taking people that are perceived as trash and turning them into treasure. Dealing a new hand of life to those who have nothing but the ability to pray for a miracle. There are so many voices that the sound is deafening.

To one day walk into a school and be surrounded by hundreds of kids who until recently were eating out of dumpsters is accomplishment to the highest degree. To one day staff a factory with hundreds of people who until then had no place to go to put food on their family's table. Take these examples and replicate them to service a bottomless demand and those prayers are being answered. With more than 50 cities having in excess of one million residents in the lesser-developed America, it only places more of an emphasis on finding real solutions to high-density urban poverty. Progress must begin where it is most difficult creating impactful results for the benefit of society as a whole.

Progress will begin with the education of the poor. Taking kids off the streets who without any help will undoubtedly become the future of drugs and prostitution in their neighborhoods. In not accepting what is considered a suitable education for the poor, we will create something that delivers actual advantages beginning with the English language. Making the kid's futures more relevant by incorporating the real world into the most effective teaching methods known today. Giving them the tools to leave the world of dire poverty and enter the functioning city wherever this may be to aptly succeed. Surrounding the kids with people who care about them and want to help them become quality people for their journey through life. Our students are our progress.

Progress will begin with not accepting conventional wisdom for how a business should operate. Achieving a positive impact on all who are involved in the journey, not just the destination. Changing the script in that factories are meant to provide for the people instead of people for the factories while still following the guidelines of capitalism. Creating the greatest and most beautiful product of all, mass employment, as through this we will take the utmost pride. Going into neighborhoods with astronomical unemployment rates and providing opportunity for those who wish for a better life torpedoing long-standing problems. Companies founded and branded around a cartoon character that represents something much more than a business but a family. Aiding people all the way out of the slums by providing livable wages and a working support network. Our employees are our progress.

Progress will begin with giving customers something more than they have grown accustomed to. Creating a greater story than anything that has come before, a spectacle of product with tangible results at the end of the performance. Listening to the customers to ensure that our products are not simply created as a hollow means to employment, but to answer the voice of what is lacking in the marketplace, both altruistically and commercially. Allowing customers to play a role in real progress through an act they were already planning on performing. Not a bond of company and customer but something stronger, more lasting and indescribable. Our customers are our progress.

Progress will begin with better serving donors. People who will hold us accountable to our commitment for not just smarter solutions, but our desire to treat them with no less respect than shareholders of a publically traded company. Exercising the unlocked potential of an endowment to not only return a percentage but also to create both a unifying voice and large-scale employment. Fashioning an online magazine to keep contact throughout the year with a global base and a destination style event that features our annual bi-lingual documentary. Maximizing the amount of donor's money that flows from A to B in a sustainable fashion enlarging the smiles on both sides. Making it easier and more appealing for those interested in visiting the actual operations to do so while enhancing themselves in the process. Our donors are our progress.

As Woody Allen once said, ninety percent of life is just showing up and we are here. This writing wasn't done to be perfect, it was done to be me. To show that adversity is the first step to truth, to inspire others with great hope, great courage, and going forward, great achievement. By boldly sharing an idea of how to change what help can be, we thus craft the stage to contribute to the advancement of the Americas. Important is not where we come from but where we are going, to mass-produce miracles.

Guns Blazin'

The real poverty being addressed is that disease and hunger are long standing effects of a lack of resources. It is an unrelenting punishment until a point is reached where a parent losing a child becomes an accident of no importance, which is the case in the lowest levels of poverty. These are results that were inherited from centuries of repression and total submission. In the slums, it is effortless to see children who by their physical statures appear eight or nine years old, but who nevertheless are thirteen or fourteen. We must be able to erase our old concepts and come ever closer to the cause and as we do, understand the value we choose to place on a human life.

There are ways to be victorious in our quest, this is done by encircling and then annihilating the problem. As this challenge is embarked upon, we will not say, "Here we are. We come to give you the charity of our presence, to teach you with our science, to demonstrate your errors, your lack of refinement, your lack of elementary knowledge." We will go with an investigative zeal and with a humble spirit, to learn from the source of wisdom that is the people. Always remaining sensitive to the struggle, the sufferings, and the hopes of the oppressed people and remember that there is a difference between under and badly developed cultures.

If one feels the world is not as perfect as it should be, then they must take the greatest weapon ever invented of technology and use it to service society. We must utilize technology to benefit the largest number of human beings possible so that we may build the society of tomorrow. What I am proposing to be done cannot be accomplished without the freshness, enthusiasm, and expertise of youth coupled with wider support. If there is no one to stand up and fight, we have no army. For this army to be assembled leaders must emerge and this is done by example. We must not worry about what to do to please others. Just do what is necessary, what seems logical at the time, and this is how leaders will influence change. Those responsible for great transformations did not see their dreams realized quickly, but eventually they triumphed. Nothing can stop history as it will always endure.

As we embark upon this quest there will be mistakes but there will never be lies. If we can enlist the help of enough people we will create a beautiful common experience that will be found to have an equal number of participants as recipients. Working together we will learn how to remove obstacles, which in turn will transform into magnificent results. This work will not be easy or quick and will require more than simply people's hands, but also that of their heads and hearts. In order to create an organization capable of tremendous force we must find our rhythm and direction. Without these things, the ideas that create momentum will begin to lose their effect. To reach our goal we have to work every day, along the lines of improving ourselves; of gaining knowledge and understanding about the world around us; of inquiring, finding out, and knowing why things are the way they are; and always considering humanity's great problems as our own.

The current generation is the vanguard and will be asked to become the generation of sacrifice. Some of these will be due to a sense of global empathy and some will be related to cleaning up after previous generations unawareness and apathy. If we are to see change it is something that must be demanded as opposed to simply requested. The best way to demand is to act. People prefer something that breaks the monotony of life as the highlights are what define us. Something every once in awhile that suddenly reminds us of our own personal worth, which is not a job title or the resulting figure of a bank account but our worth within society. Each and everyone one of us must think of how to make reality better and act upon that. Maybe it is financially supporting a cause or picking up a shovel, but being active and not simply aging as life aimlessly passes by.

There are only 24 hours in a day and 60 minutes in an hour, meaning there is always a limit to what can be done. This limit should not prevent us from wishing to accomplish all that we strive, but confirming on a daily basis the efficiency of our thought. We are beginning to plant the seeds of our efforts and these seeds must be defended and protected so that they may grow. Many of those seeds revolve around education and it is true that people can be educated at marvelous speed. Along with speed, this is an area of substance as education is the bread of the people. Education and economic development are forever destined to be married at the hip. Our efforts are meaningless if they do not result in the victory of all, and by all I mean everyone from the benefactors to the final recipients. MS+EG.

Drama King

My story begins when I was living in Buenos Aires on June 10, 2006 on what appeared a quite normal day. I was with a local gal and we were preparing to go see her family for Argentina's first game in the World Cup against the Ivory Coast. As she exited the shower in getting ready, she started talking of how she did not feel well and may not be able to go. I was excited to go and watch the *Albiceleste* play as they were a favorite to win and just assumed it was a case of a female being difficult as we really had to go. After exiting my shower, I went in front of the mirror for a shave no different than the thousand other times I had performed this act. After a few moments, I looked at my reflection with a glazed focus and noticed that my face was cut in about six places with blood gliding down. I don't know how long I stood staring in the mirror trying to figure out what was happening but eventually it did click in that something was wrong and more importantly that we needed to get out of that apartment and fast. This was the last thought I had as when I turned to move I remember my legs going out and falling, ricocheting off the bidet to the floor. This is when I died.

Contrary to what is said about these types of experiences, there is no white light and no one telling you to walk towards it. There is darkness and it closes fast. As we were unconscious in the apartment awaiting our fate, she had an asthma attack that was enough to wake her to the point where she could text her mother informing her that something was wrong and to send help. Her sister and her sister's boyfriend came to the apartment unknowing what they were to find. My fat, naked ass strewn across the bathroom floor must have made for quite the entry. I do remember a bit of being slapped really hard to which I replied by introducing myself and shaking the boyfriend's hand, not that I hadn't known him for quite a few months at that point. Then I relented again to the darkness.

After two weeks in a coma I awoke again. The reason that I was in the coma was that when I arrived to Fernandez Hospital in Palermo, the carbon monoxide level in my blood was 39.6%. How carbon monoxide kills a person is that it suffocates you from the inside by attacking the oxygen in your blood. At a later date when I was speaking to my neurologist, because everyone has a neurologist, I asked the question of what was the highest recorded level of someone surviving a carbon monoxide attack. I was told that it is not simply the level but the length of time you are unconscious and that blood does not reach your brain. I was out for around 7 hours and there was a look of astonishment on his face that I interpreted as, if I were a Catholic, this would qualify as my first miracle. The hospital put me in a drug-induced coma to try and calm my body after arriving by ambulance and gave it the only chance it had for survival, in a sense hitting the pause button on my fate. For the decisions that were made there that day, I will always be grateful as they are why I am sitting here reflecting today.

Obviously I did surface and overcame being clinically dead. When I awoke from the coma I was in such a drug induced state that I really had absolutely no idea what was going on. My family was there, my gal, and I believe her mom. I didn't have too many questions as to how I got there and more in regards to the other things that were currently going on in the room. Coming down the walls were beautiful waterfalls with murals of topless mermaids. I can see why some are such big fans of opium. I began babbling non-sense associated with the dreams I was having in my drug-induced state. This included trying to get my sister to bring me a beer from my armoire that I had been carrying with me in my most recent dream. I must have asked a good five times and if I would have received that imaginary beer, it would have been the greatest thing in the world. In hindsight, they probably could have just pretended to hand me something and I would have been happy. I had about 10 different tubes in my body keeping me alive and the doctors had given me almost no chance of living and even less to awake in any state other than that of vegetative. Looking back, I have to assume under the pretenses my family thought there was going to be no other role than taking my remains back to the States, pulse or no.

I recall awaking in intermediate care after having been transferred from intensive care. I had no idea that I was hooked to an IV of blood and tried to move only to have the IV come off its hanger into my bed. It would have been one thing if it just fell and they just hung it back but somehow the bag opened and I was lying in a pool of blood with an Argie nurse yelling at me. Needless to say I had zero clue what was going on around me, but I had a pretty good idea it was her who was going to have to clean this up. Around these times I was on about six drips of morphine a day, I really liked morphine and morphine really liked me and we became the best of friends.

The following day or so while in intermediate, I was given inventory of the condition I was in. Compartment syndrome in my right leg which is where you swell from the inside out and luckily staved off the need for having my leg filleted, a large blood clot in my left leg, both my kidneys had failed and thus I was massively swollen, sciatic nerve damage which is intensely painful, substantial nerve damage all through my lower half, lost a muscle in my left hip and couldn't control my leg which is odd to say the least, I had lost the use of my legs to atrophy, and an undiagnosed amount of brain damage. Regardless of all these effects, I was alive again.

At this time getting better wasn't any type of goal that I had, simply not thinking about the pain was sufficient enough. I had teams of doctors who would come visit on a daily basis, one team was toxicology and I can't remember what the other team was, then there were individual doctors going in and out. The machines they hooked me to were so antiquated that I could only laugh, and then I yelled once they turned them on. Some of those machines hurt like all hell, especially the ones that had to do with nerves. My Spanish was a challenge just to order pizza and have it delivered to the right address. I had at one point ordered pizza to a wrong address, something to do with the pronunciation of tres and seis but that story doesn't fit here. I had no idea what any of these doctors were saying at the time which was a bit frustrating when some of the questions revolve around if you are going to walk again but more importantly if the swelling in your balls was ever going to go away. No matter what the issue was, this was always the question I asked, probably pretty typical for a 26 year old.

I will say that it was amazing how many of the dreams from when I was in a coma came back to me. They made no sense at the time but later when I understood what was physically going on they had some basis. In one there was a group of witches who were trying to kill me and there was this child witch who kept trying to put a gas mask on my face. I remember the witches would invite people over and kill them in front of me. Another dream I was working for the Argie version of the FBI or something doing raids, in another we were at the mini-mart trying to buy water when it was overtaken by robbers and we were shot, another I remember being back in Seattle and whenever I attempted to drink something the glass would shatter and go down my throat, and the last was when I was carrying my armoire with all my beer around the city with me. This one ended with the manager of the place I was staying at tying me to a bed and not letting me go, that one was pretty messed up even in the dream like the beginning of a Tarantino movie.

Maybe it was the fact that my brain was working and thinking about something that I staved off having brain damage, I'll never know but it makes as much sense as just having a thick head. In my room was really nothing, my bed had a crank that I needed someone to help me with and an intercom that didn't work for when I wanted help with the bed. She and my family used to visit and stay in the afternoon and she used to stay through the night sleeping in a chair by my bed. I don't think I could have made it through without having her there. Not only for moral support and sanity but also as when I needed some pain or sleeping meds there was someone who was both mobile and could communicate with the doctors. I had my friends from Buenos Aires who would visit and also a great deal from her family who was quite wonderful through the entire ordeal as was mine.

I did get to see a few games of that World Cup however it was only when I was taken to dialysis which was an experience in itself. I don't think there is anything more draining then when they take 6 liters of blood out of you and only put 4 back in. I took my dialysis in the neck which apparently is uncommon in the States but I recall that I used to permanently have the cords sticking out of my neck and this used to lead to about one or two fevers daily. I would just have to sit there and take them until they broke. And to anyone who thought hospital food was bad in the States, Argie public hospital food will trump that in a day. I hated it so much they started allowing me to receive outside food because I wouldn't eat. In the end, I left the hospital around 55 pounds lighter from diet and atrophy. This may sound like a good diet recipe but its not. I lost so much weight that it used to hurt just sitting down on the toilet as it was bone on bowl.

I am quite sure this is more than enough to frame the picture of where I began in the process. I cannot tell you when but at some point when I was lying in my hospital bed unable to walk, I made myself the promise that if I ever recovered from the experience I would return to Argentina to do something good. I am not going to honestly make the claim that when I said this to myself I had any idea of what it meant. In returning to the States after a few months in the Argie public hospital, I put my blinders on the best I could to everything around me and worked as hard as I knew how to get better. I invented my own type of rehab. I did the pool therapy to learn how to walk again and would have them put those pulsating things on my feet turning it up to where I couldn't take it anymore and do 20 minutes of it. I thought this would help my nerves come back as I knew there was only a short window where they could recover significantly. I also started doing acupuncture and then when I wasn't in rehab smoked as much weed as I possibly could. Smoking didn't get rid of the pain but I didn't think about it and helped put my weight back on. This also gave me the opportunity to get off Percocet and Neurontin as I have always hated taking pills. In the end, whatever the right one was in this group or the combination is unknown to me but I do know that today I have the vast majority of my nerves back and can walk and talk like anyone else. Other than the scars on my neck from the dialysis, one would never know I went through anything like this unless I told them.

Everybody has some event along the way that internally shapes who they are and this was mine. I do know that if this had to happen, I am glad it happened when I was young so that both my body and mind could fight with the most strength I could offer. Leaving an experience like this there is no other way than to attach your mind to the things you want to take from it, which in turn enables you to leave the ones you don't in the past to the best of your ability. I left with the belief that I can accomplish absolutely anything. There are a great many people who make this claim but very few who have the track record to wholeheartedly believe it. How many times in your life do you get a chance to go through something so wrenching and come out on the other side stronger for it? Putting absolutely every piece of mettle you have behind yourself to accomplish one thing and emerge victoriously. The experience tore through everything I thought my life was and forced me to start again.

For the last couple of years, I have been hard thinking about this charity and what exactly it is that I want it to do. The dream behind it is large but one I have no doubts that I will be able to fulfill it if I can push myself hard and long enough where enough people will say "yes". I'd like to tell you that I chose Argentina, but the reality is that Argentina chose me. This story encompasses a formal introduction to my charity, Hijos de Argentina.

Motion of the Ocean

In order to understand more of where we are, I have to take you back to a different beginning. When I received my tax-exempt status from the IRS, I was on a plane two weeks later to Argentina to get everything moving. I have no doubt that I did this the exact opposite way when compared to how most go about starting their charity. Most would have already had their partners on the ground organized that they were going to work with and then go through the proper channels for obtaining certification but not me. I guess I saw it as adding to the adventure having to go down there with my broken Spanish and in the course of five days with never having been to Rosario, force myself to perform. I still recall at the end of the visit standing on the roof of the hostel and looking out over the city filled with pride at what I had accomplished. No one in his or her right mind should spend 8 months working on getting all the paperwork complete and then visit their city for the first time in a make or break fashion, but that's what I did and I wouldn't have changed anything. If you know all the details of the future then what is the point in living the present?

I entered Rosario a day ahead of my friend from Buenos Aires who was helping me with translating and getting about. When I arrived, I went to visit the local churches thinking that this was a good place to start but it was quite dejecting to witness how unhelpful they were. After I was literally about to give up hope on this process having had no luck in quite a few places, my friend was able to get us a meeting arranged with the local representative from the Salvation Army through a family member. We sat down with the rep and I told him the stories of what had happened to me, why I was in Rosario, and what I was trying to do. I was a bit surprised to hear how limited their operations were in Rosario with its large presence in the States but this made them all the more attractive with the same name recognition back home where I had to fundraise.

In our meeting it became evident to me that the way to get started without question was to partner with someone who was already on the ground and I liked the things he told me they were doing to help. I had dreams from the beginning of building up an operation with our own people but it is important to know the difference between fiction and reality in real-time circumstances. We spoke in detail about some of the challenges for the kids living in the slums and I told him about my hopes and some of the things I wanted to accomplish. I'll always remember having a conversation with him about how people from that country simply don't dream that big. I told him that people from mine don't either and we got along just fine after better understanding one another.

After driving through Rosario which has a very industrial feel, we made it to the other side of the train tracks marking the city border to the suburb of Perez. We were there to visit a camp they sponsored in order to understand if this was the type of first project I was looking for. It's probably not fair for me to judge the quality of the camp as for the kids it is something that they look forward to all year. Where they have the opportunity to get out of the slums and play for a week forgetting about all the challenges of home. There was a pool, a soccer field, play equipment, dorms, a kitchen, and a chapel. I asked the rep with Salvation Army being a Christian organization, what it is they teach in the religious studies and he told me hope. I had no problem with this answer as it is something these kids need in spades.

I was there in particular to see the beds and mattresses along with the condition of a few other things. The camp sleeps around 80 with more or less four rooms sleeping 20 per. The mattresses were in such bad condition and probably never had a great deal of quality to them to begin. Springs poking out, the majority were torn and stained. To me, this represented a great first project for Hijos and I committed to buy new beds and mattresses. I don't think they ever expected to see me again but I knew I would be seeing them.

About a year later I came back with the money I had fundraised for them. I hadn't started on the charity full time yet and there was nothing easy about fundraising in Seattle to help the poor in Rosario. Originally I was looking at doing strictly beds but after returning and talking with the camps manager, it was decided that some balance was the best option. I asked them to tell me what the best use was for the funds I had raised and in the end we purchased some new mattresses, provided scholarships to attend the camp as hard times were all around, and repairs to the girls bathroom that was not in working order. In returning after a year I had a good idea what it was I wanted to do larger picture in Rosario having logged a great many hours thinking about the city and project. I followed up on some questions that could only be answered in the city such as real estate prices along with procedure but most important was spending more time in the slums. It is not really the type of place that one can just pop into with any safety associated but after finishing our project with the camp there were some people who volunteered to take me about.

I had concluded that the biggest obstacle to my fundraising was the fact I didn't have anything visual to work around. There was no way that I could simply waltz in and click away taking pictures but I had an idea. My idea was to purchase 20 disposable cameras and pass them out having the kids photograph their own area. After completing the initial project it got me some credibility and I used it to have this done. The project was an incredible success and was conducted at ground zero in the exact slum that I wish to begin. The instructions that I gave with the cameras was to pass them out to some kids who lived in a Villa Gobernador Galves slum to photograph family, friends, and normal life. The pictures came back giving me insight into the slum that I couldn't have gotten in fifty visits. When outsiders come in and photograph everyone looks so desolate but when family takes the shots they are different. There are smiles, laughter, and a true reflection of how people live regardless of possession. It shows that they are human just like everyone one else and not merely a charity case.

I selected the best 81 photographs and around individual 4"x 6" frames, worded the direction of the charity as reflected below.

(1) Henry Ford in his wisdom stated that, "If people go into business with the idea (2) that they are going to serve the public and their

employees as well as themselves, they would be (3) assured of success at the very start." My dream is to find that success for my charity (4) venture. The way to help people in the present is employment and for the future is (5) education. To realize the trifecta, a charity owned subsidiary must be implemented to act as (6) the bridge between charity and commerce. Once these three are working in unison the potential (7) is limitless. The centerpiece of the vision is the ability to mass-produce schools for the poor in (8) South America while creating employment as a byproduct. Our model is in Rosario, Argentina. The initial (9) criteria called for a city with a population over 1 million and a deep-sea port. For the structures we (10) are going to purchase available warehouses. It is a flexible structure to work with and (11) consistently available in large cities. These structures are cost-efficient and provide the (12) needed utility connections while presenting a green solution to education. With high ceilings (13) a second floor can be added for dimes on $'s versus finished real estate. These are solid (14) assets for the charity to own going forward and can be used as collateral in times of survival. (15) Using warehouses allows us to deal in the largest number of kids possible and is designed with (16) sleeping quarters upstairs from classrooms. The schools will be bi-lingual and open to young (17) kids with no home. The idea is to give these kids a fair shot at success in life through a (18) clean, well-crafted slate. The English speaking staff come as paying volunteers through already (19) established programs such as gap-year and will help subsidize operational costs. The native (20) English side will be a positive influence bringing in educated teachers, keeping class sizes (21) down, creating language fluency, and offering a potentially rich reward to volunteers. The (22) remainder of the staff is permanent and local to insure stability. Workforce stability is created (23) with funds managed in the States and converted late with a strong dollar belief. The curriculum (24) will be developed with the highest quality of information available ensuring our best efforts. (25) Once we have our educational model size is only a number on a multiplication chart. If David (26) slayed a dwarf instead of a giant, would anyone have cared? Donors today are more sophisticated (27) than ever and are salivating for something new. A charity owned company is nothing more than (28) an LLC with 100% ownership through the registered 501(c)3 making it a wholly owned subsidiary. (29) We are making a head on run at tapping into something special as this market is enormous. With (30) a charity owned business there is no exit strategy so the long-term goals are what we build towards. (31) On the business side that point is long-term job creation behind velocity economics but there is (32) a lot of ground to cover to understand how this is possible. The logo for the brand is a (33) cartoon character of a smiling, fat, happy, blue cow. His name is Bluedo and he's based on some (34)

Argentine slang that "loosely" means good friend. With Bluedo the idea is to create a brand (35) that is associated with charity and trusted product. Our first product is wine in South Florida and a (36) nice representation of Argentina. Wine is the perfect product to begin with as not only does it (37) open a global marketplace but it gives the charity a voice. It is a method for us to communicate (38) with customers in a friendly manner over a bottle of high-quality Malbec under $15. The consumer (39) venture is of incredible importance to understand if the economics work and planning becomes clearer. (40) Our first venture is tough but the wine business can best be observed as having a full basement yet plenty (41) of room upstairs and we got the key. Miami is our first wine market and the heart of the Latin (42) community where we will be based. Our global sales would represent different consumer markets (43) working together through a voluntary process to build schools in places of need, no small feat. (44) There is no real logic to how international markets are developed which really plays to our (45) advantage of being new and timing the back side of a recovery with a new brand. Some huge margins (46) are out there if we can find good distribution cause there is no one telling the same story as (47) we are in any language. The wine will determine which markets are open to the brand going forward. (48) The job venture is a vertically integrated leather goods company. After touring the States

(49) doing market research on leather goods there is no question that this market is more than available (50) to a young, classic Argentine style. The country is known for quality leather and is a (51) major player in the rawhide export industry with Italy as their main customer but (52) limited in their domestic craftsmanship. The bag assembly would be staffed through job- (53) training programs in the slums as craftsmanship can be taught meaning we would not require (54) previous education or experience. Present would be a loyal and trainable workforce who (55) would jump at quality legal opportunity to put food on their table. The more product we (56) sell the more jobs we will create through volume economics, basic theory but not so basic (57) application. Our real industry is job creation but we need an outlet and manufacturing can (58) create an incredible number of jobs. You may even see us try and do our part in spreading (59) the game of baseball in South America. We do not need containers of product to get people (60) excited to buy online as there are many outlets for visibility. Later on we will purchase (61) live cattle to better control our leather quality but also we can use the beef to feed our kids, (62) keep costs down for everyone, and produce more jobs. The second company would finalize our model as now (63) we can convert the schools back to warehouses for the manufacturing jobs and begin construction (64) on a new school creating more zero education jobs. We stretch our funds as far as they (65) can

go by raising dollars, producing for pesos, selling for dollars, and returning profits to (66) disburse in pesos. The advice being followed is that we can use our brains to lay a plan (67) but we will shift to reason upon its execution as the plan will constantly change with (68) changing conditions, that's making a mess of Rockefeller but nonetheless understandable. (69) Kids in a slum we work with took the photos for this project and we would like to extend (70) our deepest thanks for helping. We passed the cameras to the kids with the instructions (71) to photograph normal life and this is what they brought back. These neighborhoods (72) are beyond dangerous and if an outsider goes in with a camera they certainly would (73) not be going out with it. The kids see a place of happiness regardless of how bad it (74) really is. At this point in their life growing up in a slum, they see the world no different (75) than any other kid. Kissinger's analogy is useful in the conventional army loses if it does (76) not win. The guerrilla army wins if it does not lose. In knowing that we cannot win our (77) strategy is to fight and not lose. High density urban poverty has no form so the only way to (78) fight is through economic example. These ideas are potentially disruptive to today's (79) marketplace but the goal is clear. We are going to build a very large happy family. A family (80) of students, employees, suppliers, retailers, donors, customers, and anyone else who wishes to (81) become involved in what we are doing. This is my dream and my business plan.

Double Deez

I've always been a believer that if you cannot break something down to its most simplistic form then you truly do not understand what it is that you are doing. The most simplistic way to understand something is visually. Everything I will work towards explaining is the result of breaking down the following basic graph, the double diamond.

The key point to the double diamond is where all efforts feed and the belief in the creation of opportunity, downhill running. This is a formula that is so simple that it very well may be plausible. Einstein said everything should be made as simple as possible but not one bit simpler. The double diamond is our E=MC squared.

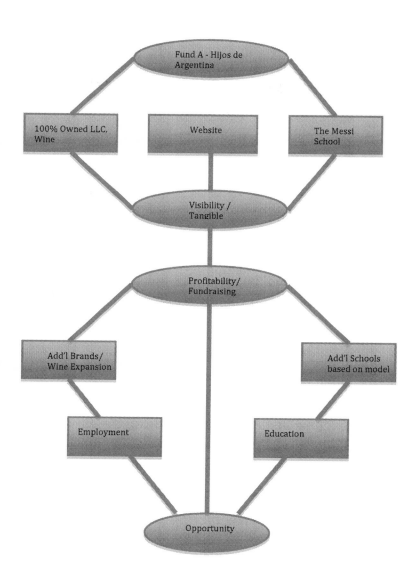

The Spot

Location is the most important factor for this style of charity. With the wrong location, we could not do a fraction of the things we have set out to accomplish. If you were to ask me what the parameters were before researching, the list would have been something in relation to; mid-high population, public universities, culture, infrastructure, poverty level, and a place that I could handle spending an extensive amount of time. Rosario was the first city that I began to research and I was sold by the end of the process even through I had never been there prior. When I was last back in Buenos Aires, I told my friends what I was doing and they couldn't understand why I would want to help Rosario and not Buenos Aires. The problem with Buenos Aires was that I could never wrap my head around where the city began and where it stopped. In a country with 40MM people, 14MM live in or around Buenos Aires.

Rosario is located at latitude -33 and longitude -60 placing it about 3-4 hours to the North/Northwest of Buenos Aires. It has a city population of roughly 1MM with its metro area bringing the total to 1.4MM people. The city has an affluent portion to its population due to trade and commodities yet 23.4% of the city resides underneath the poverty line. The dollar figure for the poverty line was recently raised to $2/day, which would correspond to some 330k+ people with metro considered. It is the third largest city in terms of population and is second in terms of importance. It is home to the countries largest commodities market as well as the largest futures market. It represents the center of the country's fiber optic ring as well as being where General Manuel Belgrano created the first flag of Argentina.

Rosario is a low bank city situated on the Parana River. The river acts as the spine for the region and Rosario sits at the mouth of it. The strategic location is destined to become a significant transportation hub growing its already dominant position in the region. It is a bi-oceanic corridor that links Rio Grande do Sul in Brazil on the Atlantic Ocean to Valparaiso, Chile on the Pacific Ocean, an important component in global distribution and the core center of Mercosur, the common market for South America. It is a port city second in volume only to Buenos Aires and represents the heart of the agriculture and cattle industries hence the aforementioned trading markets. A more detailed list of exports include wheat, flour, soy, linseed, corn, sugar, lumber, meats, and wool. The port was recently drudged and now acts as a 34ft deep-water port. This depth is important as it can facilitate cargo vessels of up to 50 tonnes and the port is very accessible requiring no tugs.

In keeping with their infrastructure, the international airport was recently refurbished to work with cargo and offers direct flights to every major city in the Southern Cone. Rosario acts as a hub for major over land transport with 1.1MM passengers a month and 784 national and international routes. It also offers an extensive network of roadways as well as being the railroad terminal for NE Argentina. A bullet train was even proposed and approved by the national government that was to go from Buenos Aires-Rosario-Cordoba, which has since been shelved due to economic restrictions. This all goes to show that the city has an infrastructure that can support any company and/or endeavor.

There are several museums including fine arts, decorative arts, historical, provincial, city, contemporary, natural sciences, as well as local destinations such as a planetarium, observatory, and many theatres varying in size and function. Soon to be added to the list will be the theatre known as Puerto de la Musica, which is targeted for completion in 2010 by renowned modern architect Oscar Niemeyer of Brazil and projects to be one of the most important theatres in all of Latin America. I like the idea that there is so much culture here that would allow for kids from the slums to be exposed to anything and everything given the opportunity. The city has a couple golf courses in the Rosario Golf Club and The Jockey Club, though neither are destination quality they fulfill their purpose.

Rosario is an important educational center on a national and international level. The National University of Rosario is public and consists of twelve schools, three preparatory academies, and is comprised of over 75,000 students. The other public university in Rosario is the National Technological School and has eight different engineering focuses though much smaller. Also in the city are seven private universities but these are irrelevant to our approach as the state owned educational facilities are free to its residents.

Rosario was the birthplace of three of Argentina's most famous and influential citizens. This list includes Antonio Berni, the country's most renowned artist and it should be noted that he did a series dealing with children from the slums making him recognizable around the world; Juanito Laguna, slum child, and Ramona Montiel, a prostitute. A sad note in regards to Berni is that in '08 a truck transporting fifteen of his most famous works of art between museums was robbed in Buenos Aires. I was actually in the city when it happened to which the government issued reports that the robbers probably had no idea what they were stealing, two men were murdered in the process. I believe Berni to be a vastly under appreciated artist outside of Argentina having had a unique style giving a voice to the people who had none. His style of surrealism did not resemble Miro's or Dali's but was uniquely his own. Berni even at one point in the 30's worked in Rosario's town hall.

Ernesto "Che" Guevarra was born in Rosario to a middle class family of Spanish-Irish decent. Best known for his participation in the Cuban Revolution his tale did not end happily being assassinated by the C.I.A. in Bolivia. A controversial figure in history, Guevarra lived an

31

adventurous life and his death in Bolivia created a legend that still lives. He is a hero in Rosario and they recently erected a statue in his honor though not comparable in magnitude to the memorial in Santa Clara, Cuba. One of the most visited locations in Rosario is where Guevarra was born though since converted into a hostel. An interesting person when viewed through the words of his speeches delivered in Cuba having an immaculate understanding of the common person. I will not state that I agree with all of his actions but there was never a lack of heart involved.

The third person of notable fame, and the only living, is Lionel Messi. He is arguably the world's top soccer player having recently been awarded the Ballon d'or and FIFA Player of the Year. This is a result of leading his club, FC Barcelona, to six various titles the previous year and large expectations have been placed on his 22 year old shoulders to lead Argentina to World Cup glory. If you are someone who likes sports it is difficult not to follow soccer in Argentina with this being the only game in town, more or less a religion when all is said and done. I knew from this that Messi was from Rosario and also used to play for my favorite club when a child, Newell's Old Boys. There is currently large contingency of young Argentine talent from Rosario playing for Europe's top clubs; Messi (Barcelona), Maxi Rodriguez (Liverpool), Gabriel Heinze (Marseille), Ángel Di María (Benefica), Ezequil Garey (Real Madrid), Caesar Delgado

(Lyon), Ezequil Lavezzi (Napoli), and Éver Banega (Valencia).

In Argentina, they are notorious for problems of corruption in their government as are many parts of the developing world. When I was living there, someone told me that winning election to public office was the equivalent to that of winning the lottery. The previous mayor of Rosario was a man named Hermes Binner who goes against this reputation. Mr. Binner was recognized by the UN for the service he had done for his city during his 8 years as mayor. One of the most important things that Mr. Binner accomplished was to decentralize the operations of the city into 6 large administrative districts. This allowed for better citizen rule and less bureaucracy. In regards to myself coming in and looking to help slums in Rosario, it makes it much more palatable when I can begin in one of the districts and work out from there.

Mr. Binner placed a large emphasis on the public and was recognized by the Pan-American Health Organization for his health plan that was deemed to be a model for the rest of Latin America. On top of these things, he understood the economic and sociopolitical importance working towards increasing Rosario's stature within Mercosur. The current mayor is Miguel Lifshitz who served in a variety of cabinet positions including Public Services Secretary for Rosario and was hand selected by Mr. Binner. Binner is currently the governor of the Santa Fe province where he went after reaching his term limit as mayor and is considered to be a frontrunner for the next Argentine presidential election in October 2011.

Rosario offers us as many advantages as we can conceptually hope to attain. Logistically relevant as well as culturally, a large city but not an overwhelming one, this is where we are aiming to call our home away from home. By being location focused it allows us to form long lasting relationships, people will know us and we will know them. They will know what we stand for and what we are there hoping to accomplish. It would be impossible to build a strong foundation with a nomadic cause. I don't want to go in there and help educate people just so that they can sit with their educations in their hands and not know how to apply it. I want to be in a place where I can witness the people I help succeed and Rosario offers this potential.

Purgatory

What exactly is an Argie slum or villa miseria? The direct translation of a villa miseria would be "miseryville", not the nicest sounding place but this is also for good reason. A typical makeup of who is living in a slum consists of migrant workers coming from poorer provinces or from impoverished rural areas near cities, immigrants coming from Bolivia and Paraguay, local citizens who have fallen from an already precarious economic position, but it is primarily comprised of those born in the slums who have been unable to rise out. The different groups typically do not mix and live in pockets next to pockets. An example of a large pocket are the Tobas who are native descendants coming to Rosario from the Chaco region.

All in there are about 2MM slum dwellers in Argentina and this figure is growing rapidly with the current economic conditions bringing in large numbers from rural settings. The slums vary greatly in size and layout with some ranging from only a few hundred residents to some encompassing tens of thousands. Around greater Buenos Aires, there are roughly 640 physical slum locations which would probably place Rosario somewhere in the 50-75 range. This emphasizes very early why it is so important to create a program that is readily transferrable being able to implement the model from city to city and slum to slum. These slums are located around large urban centers and traditionally the only way out of them is either through soccer, music, or marriage; not great odds.

The slums are thought of as havens for drug dealers, prostitutes, and thieves which is true but this only represents a small percentage of their residents. There are a great many quality people who would like nothing more than some help in either making for a better environment to live or guidance in how to get themselves and their families to a better place. Some have made their way out to find work but it is one of those situations where they cannot give their address because having a residence in a slum carries such a stigmatism, truly the bottom of their caste system. Back around the turn of the century, these locations were used as transient places where primarily Spanish and Italian immigrants would stay temporarily before moving on after getting their bearings with no shame associated. Over the years and as the economic problems compounded, it became permanent housing for all of the residents.

High-density urban poverty is a term to describe the living conditions where the structures are wall to wall. When there is not enough space to continue they will begin to stack vertically. These locations must be thought of as the epicenter of where efforts must be focused to have an effect on poverty, the collecting ground for all problems. There is nowhere else for these people to go and no funds available to get there. For every person who can make their way out there are two to three coming in to take their place with no end in sight. As a true bottom it offers stability for our programs to exist because people will always be there.

The realities of this life are harsh and if it's not understood then it is impossible to convey to someone the importance of what we are setting out to do. A typical family living in a slum is a couple with 3-4 kids, 5.4 total household. In a family of five or more there is usually only room for at the most four in a bed and the remaining children must sleep on the floor. These types of structures have dirt floors that a mattress is placed upon. The most common type of dwelling in a slum is comprised of two rooms with one being for sleeping and one for living. The males who are fortunate to obtain work are in factories, construction, and as cartoneros (people who go through the trash to collect cardboard and then sell it for recycling). The majority of women do not work and stay at home to raise their family. The ones who work do so primarily as housekeepers and in the occasional textile factory. A fair guess for the unemployment rate in a neighborhood such as this would be 65-70% and this figure includes black market employment. This percentage would reflect a number four times the current rate of Flint, Michigan. The most common employment is sporadic in the form of gathering for protests or rallies that they will receive a few pesos to participate in.

The kids for the most part do not attend school. Even though public school has no cost to attend it is the costs around attendance that prove to be the largest deterrent. There is no money for transportation, uniforms, supplies, or books making it near impossible for the kids to follow up on this pursuit. The ones who are able to attend will find an education that is significantly below what is offered to their fellow countrymen. The women will work hard to do their best to keep their children headed to school but as there is a lack of structure to households it proves difficult to force the kids to attend. People attempt to send their kids to live with others outside of the slums so that they may have the chance of getting out but people aren't exactly lining up to help.

Typically when the kids wake up in the morning they leave their houses to go out amongst friends in their neighborhood. Sometimes returning for lunch but many do not have lunch available at home and will eat from whatever they can find in the streets or possibly make a few pesos begging or washing windows. Many kids play soccer in the day as even with few fields in urban centers they typically find a way in the soccer crazy country. Kids today in the slums begin with drugs on the early side around the age of 8 which is also true for child prostitution. Obtaining alcohol proves difficult but drugs are much easier to obtain. At a young age the easiest drugs to find are marijuana and glue to inhale. This is the powder glue that is used when building with cinder block that can be inhaled for a high but at the cost of severely stunting ones brain. It is a very scary thought but this is also when kids start robbing as it is easier to learn to steal then it is to learn to work regardless of age. Drugs progress towards paco (similar to crack) in the teenage years. Once they are on paco it is over as they will be dead in six months and Argentina has an epidemic currently that rivals NYC in the 80's.

Most of the men who work can read and write as Argentina's literacy rate is reported as above 97.2% placing the slums in the 75% range, arguably. I would be apt to believe something around 35-50% of the residents in the slums never attended school for any length past the age of 8. The men who do work engage with their hands but a great many do not have a desire to work. Those who do not work spend most of their time around the neighborhood doing things like sitting at the corner store and watching what is happening in the local area. A problem with the ones who do work is that not enough of their earnings are returned to the family. The women are in charge of the kids and with no money it is difficult to fill basic necessities. There is a great deal of violence in married couples with drinking and extra-marital affairs the primary culprits. Many of the men have a girlfriend as well as a wife and many of the married women find themselves in extra-marital affairs as well. Separation is very uncommon in this part of society based around the factors of religion and simply that there is no place else to go. Medicine is almost non-existent and even though the hospitals claim to be free to the people, there are nuances so that this does not prove true beginning with the cost of transportation. Typically the only time people from these neighborhoods visit a hospital is in a life or death situation or for a pregnancy.

Slum life is made better by creating jobs and it is just as simple as that. From an economic standpoint creating employment will provide injections of capital to the wanting residents of these neighborhoods. Money is the key to most every problem in the slum and though we can only do so much it is of great importance and will have a resonating effect. Cash in households without strings will do everything from lesson domestic violence to help kids attend school for a longer period. One of the largest effects it will have is to create additional employment. Capital goes through more hands in these environments by a rate of 3-5x versus the world where using banks qualifies as the norm. We will see new jobs come to fruition such as vendors, though not well paying or legal, it does represent progress and it is my unsubstantiated belief that we will bring about 1.5-2.5 new jobs for every factory job created. The invisible hand can and will work.

Welcome to a place where the dogs of the rich eat better than the children of the poor.

Future (Steve) Jobs

Establishing a boarding school format is an all-encompassing commitment. We will alter the entire course of the kids lives by changing the environment and redirecting their path towards something positive. The age that is in the most need is between 4-6 or the equivalent of kindergarten to begin residency and schooling. This age represents a defining time for this particular group as decisions have been made beyond their control in regards to their fate and this is when opportunity is most needed to surface. The opportunity we can present is for students of sound mind and health. We are not entering to compete for kids but to provide a needed outlet finding much more demand than anything we can supply in the foreseeable future. Those in the greatest need of opportunity will be directed our way from the community but we are not in direct competition with any entity, built strictly to assist local government and families.

In Argentina, the one job skill that can almost guarantee employment is the ability to speak fluent English. Whether it is to work in retail, tourism, or call centers, the need is great and only getting larger as the world gets smaller. With Rosario being a port city, the more employable skill set we can create the better the chances will be at survival and staying out of the slums. Even if the kids were to decide that they do not want to finish their studies with us, by teaching English at a very early age it will be something that they take with them. Bi-lingual schools do exist in Argentina, primarily in Buenos Aires, however it is an opportunity that only those with money have the chance to receive. Bringing in native English speakers would make the international bi-lingual education stronger than most anything available currently in the country at any price. When coupling the foreign language basis with graduates in education and psychology from the university in Rosario, we are building something sound. A balanced, young, and energetic staff is assembled which is necessary for the challenges involved with this particular group of students.

Beginning at the age of a kindergarten student follows whatever the logic was when M.S. Hershey decided upon a similar format and had success. Kids of this age have the chance to leave their past behind them and readily make changes that will quickly become habit. This is young enough that I hope we can reach them before experiences with drugs or sexual abuse. The teaching of a foreign language to a young student is positive as their brains are much more accepting to its application and the language in turn will help develop other positive mental attributes. They would have had no exposure to prior formal learning and we have the perfect opportunity to start from a blank slate and provide the best education we are capable. The earlier we begin to teach and develop minds, the more intellectual capacity and higher levels we will be able to attain.

The most relevant teaching from an early age is problem solving and fostering curiosity. This is quite easy to implement into a curriculum and one that pays a great many dividends as life progresses. They must learn to fend and think for themselves as we will not be with them forever. There is not a great deal to be gained producing book smart students who outside of their academics are otherwise worthless. By giving an education that is broad enough to teach the kids to learn for themselves yet narrow enough to encompass the relevant skills and subjects, we will give everything.

There will be books, supplies, uniforms, food, and shelter but this doesn't state the half of it. Offering an education that promotes everything from technology to philosophy to athletics we will be creating something most unique. A humanities based education around a Platonic approach will be the cornerstone of development throughout the early years. In Rosario, there is opportunity to learn outside of school and offer trips to such things as Newell's soccer matches, museums, the planetarium, the beach, and many others. In a sense, creating the most normal childhood for the students who come through our doors with food for every meal and a staff that genuinely cares about their well-being.

How far the kids go in school will be based on the environment we create. If they are taught from a young age that it is expected of them and through studies is how they will earn praise, they will not know another way. Kids when they are growing will do almost anything for praise and rewards with this being something that we can readily provide and encourage. If we can open the students world and expose them to the benefits of learning, we will witness their satisfaction and few things are more rewarding. Making learning enjoyable is our largest academic task. Children's minds are so open and if they come to us at a very young age, they will not have any preconceived notions of what they can or cannot do but instead will be open to the optimism and opportunity which Hijos can offer.

We are going to provide schooling from K-5th grade and depending on the results and realities, possibly through 8th. At some point we will transition the kids to public school and our role to strictly boarding. As the kids go through school it will be obvious which are destined for more academics and which are not. For those who do not have an interest in school, I don't believe it prudent to keep trying to force a square peg in a round hole. Instead we will look at doing things such as arranging for apprenticeships so that job skills can be acquired whether they are as a mechanic, a carpenter, or a hair stylist it really doesn't matter. Just so long as when they outgrow the need for us they are able to go on with their lives and live as normally as one could expect outside of the slums. We will offer every ounce of support to our kids both while they are a resident and after they are finished. If we can help and our help is requested, we will.

In the end, it is up to us to create an atmosphere where learning is exciting and rewarding. Once kids take advantage of the learning offered to them we must do more in assisting with the first step after school to ensure the maximum opportunity for success. Education without the reality of employment is in all seriousness a detriment to its recipients. In the creation of opportunity, we are helping through basic economic and educational principles that have been proven for centuries. If I did not believe this could be done, I would not spend my time trying to build schools.

Industrial Swagger

The property transformation is key not only to the first school but in understanding what the parameters are for going forward. There are three realistic options one can look at for the structure of a school. The easiest and least realistic is the purchase of an old school, the second and most expensive option is to construct a school from scratch, while the third and most cost effective option is a remodel. The third option allows the needed flexibility to do something our own way and add a unique slant. Creativity is what is needed to address this outstanding problem and the solutions are all around. The structure that holds all the answers is the Plain Jane, abundant in every city, utility connected, warehouse.

The question remains how do we drive down costs even further. If we want to purchase a large space there is a premium that must be paid for finished real estate in any market. The most effective conclusion is adding a second floor that will provide us an additional 50-75% of square footage for less than half the finished retail price. In consulting with people who do this in the US market and make considerable profit in the process, this idea should prove fruitful on a variety of levels. The first is that it enhances the value of our real estate upon completion but more importantly it adds the needed square footage by best utilizing our available capital. Warehouses provide even more benefits when looking into the negotiation process. Every city with a population over 1M will have a plethora of warehouses. As economies grow more are built and as economies shrink more become vacant, but in either case they are available boding well for what we are aiming to accomplish throughout cycles.

In looking for a structure to house a minimum of 50 kids and the hope of 2-3 classes in total, we require large space. Not simply large space but flexible space inside and out. Not being required to be in the center of town we can push towards the outskirts which will accomplish two main things in lowering our cost per square foot but also making it more feasible to obtain a larger parcel of land. Utility connections are required and I would prefer not to be next to a slum but these are quite easy requirements to accommodate. This allows us to be patient in the process and examine quite a few properties to see what will work best for us as well as allowing ourselves to negotiate for the best possible value. Most all cities are small when it comes down to things such as warehouse owners, but when taking basic supply and demand into account we can find good value. There is a strong correlation between the price of real estate in a particular city and the amount of available employment opportunity. Meaning if we want the kids to have the greatest chance at success then some investment must be made in the structure.

For me there is no better structure to obtain than one that is spacious and has no limits to its flexibility. Its like a blank canvas that we can approach and maneuver to the benefit of our needs. The two largest obstacles in the remodel have nothing to do with adding an additional floor as it is straightforward but with the washroom and the kitchen. We have different requirements than the typical warehouse client in that we need showers and places where kids can go to wash up but the place for this is outside. Building an unattached washroom and tapping into the utilities is significantly cheaper than a larger remodel to the structure as well as being easier to replicate. In regards to the kitchen, I have decided not to build one. In looking at the costs and future use of the property, if we were to do a massive remodel in regards to a kitchen it makes no sense. A kitchen means amongst other costs a cook, supplies, groceries, and many unforeseen problems. It is much cheaper and more efficient to outsource the meals to local restaurants under contracts and have them bring in buffet style meals. This is good business for the restaurants plus the kids get not only quality prepared food, but variety. This idea resonates with me even greater as a way to positively strengthen relationships with local commerce on behalf of the school and readily adjust to large swings in numbers of attendees.

The school will require dorm space, classrooms, offices, dining, living area/rec space, and bathrooms. In looking at how to wall off space there is no need to take these walls to the ceiling but to define the space. The added second floor will be for dormitories. The outer walls of the second floor will prevent accidents but cannot feasibly reach the high ceiling. The warehouse should come with a few offices finished and the additional ones will reflect the same treatment as the classrooms and common spaces. The walls will not be permanent but movable so that spaces can keep the maximum amount of flexibility. This will allow the school to function without definition. If it is raining outside and we want to set up a game of soccer inside we can, truly anything. The space outside will be used for play areas but also where we can set up picnic tables under a tent for classes and additional space. If in the future we are presented with the possibility of constructing a new school, we can readily convert the space back to a warehouse for manufacturing or storage with the expanded usable space.

The work to be done with an architect is minimal as well as the amount of approvals needed from the city for the remodel. We will work in unison with the city before purchasing any space to make sure zoning is agreeable or amendable with housing the kids at the suburban industrial location. A contractor will be needed for the second floor, washroom, exterior basic teacher lodging, and additional lighting/outlets but these are not areas of incredible expense. Especially when taking into account the instant value being returned by the increase of usable square footage. I love the idea of having a big industrial style school as it can be extraordinary. Many new ideas can be incorporated that are not feasible in the normal school setting. Cutting garage doors into the sides so that we can effectively vent the property and open the property finding more usable space. How happy would a kid be if they could take a slide from the bedroom down to where breakfast is being served? Movie nights projected on large walls and when classes incorporate videos it takes on a whole new element, imagine a 20ft. tall Big Bird. I just hope it's enough to captivate those tiny attention spans.

Regardless of how the conceptual process comes together the fact does not change that the property transformation is the keystone to everything. A place that is flexible and works within our budget for a new school is what must be fostered. Our creativity will save us trucks of money while at the same time shaping a most unique place for kids to have a brilliant childhood.

Planes, Trains, and Automobiles

Beyond the physical structure of the school and child development related content, there still remain obstacles to finish a potentially great school on a minimal budget. The more we can do to lesson the needed operating capital the more success the larger vision will have. Instead of complaining about the difficulties related, it should be seen as a platform to incorporate new ways of barter and opportunity creation. Delving local begins with establishing programs to create jobs for people from the slums, bringing in top notch local teachers, cultivating a burgeoning volunteer tourism industry, and relying upon our English speaking staff and visitors to willingly pay fees.

After the physical structure for the school has been completed the next task is in furnishing the school. When looking at how to furnish a school for young kids the costs are not centered around technology and computers but in furniture. In a boarding school environment taking into consideration the number of kids we are preparing for there is need for a good amount of desks, chairs, tables, beds, dressers, and bookshelves to begin. This is a perfect need as not only is it reoccurring with each new class of students but also it presents an opportunity to introduce ourselves to the slums. Long term it is our aim to begin job-training programs in the slums geared towards those looking for work and there is no time like the present to begin.

Furniture making is a job that requires not much more than someone able with their hands and a desire to work. These are straightforward initial jobs to establish and also act as marketing for the schools as these people reside in the same places we are seeking kids from. Word will spread.

We will learn more about how to progress with larger job-training programs by getting our start in the neighborhoods as early as possible than with the finest consultants in the world. In our case the experts do not sit behind a desk but are sitting around wondering how they will feed their families and when opportunity will become available to them. We are not creating baseless employment for people as we are keeping our costs down in the process of furnishing the school. Incorporating the local community gives the school a greater impact as the more hands that contribute to its completion, the more real it becomes. Important is the establishment of credibility in the slums and this is not easy or available for purchase. We do not require any stage for grandstanding or promises but will quietly enter and begin to create opportunity. No need to speak but silently produce for those who are in need. Putting food on people's tables in exchange for labor is what we seek and the furnishing of our first school.

After the school nears completion the assembly of our local teachers becomes the priority. The benefit of Rosario being a large city and having its own university is that we do not have to go far to recruit. Initially we are seeking two full time teachers for the school and are looking for teachers directly out of university. What this does primarily is that we do not have to reprogram teachers in how they go about their craft. It will take a bit to explain the logic and application of using scripted curriculum but nothing overly difficult. The administrative work is nothing so difficult that it cannot be shared between two teachers to begin. I will pay a 50% premium over what the going rate is for local teaching jobs, at current exchange this premium is over $400/month. This will allow us to choose who we think proves the best fit versus settling for what is available. Instead of recruiting teachers from the education program I will look for them in the psychology department as dealing with the kids issues when they come to us is paramount. Making sure their mental wellbeing is addressed from day one will get everyone moving in unison from an earliest stage. Bringing in good teachers is expensive but not nearly as expensive as what bringing in bad ones would be.

The other portion to our permanent staff is in a support role. I would like to bring in a house mom whose job it is to make sure that everything non-education related runs smooth. Food on the tables, laundry washed, getting on the kids to do their chores, etc. and this position will not be needed in the mornings so that the teachers can work normal hours. The mom will be present in the afternoons and evenings when there is more recreation time and the type of supervision changes. To accompany the house mom there is a need for a maintenance/security/driver role. It is my hope to find a married couple for these two jobs. This would mean they will be with us for a long time and to ensure stability I will rent them a house as close to the school as possible making this job very appealing. Some teachers will come and go over time but this couple will be permanent and the resident experts of the school. The couple will be sought from the slums and will go to someone who we know and helped us leading up to the completion of the school. Having a couple from the slums will provide a connection to the kid's roots and better aid the transition.

Local staffing provides much stability to the school but it is through the English staffing that intrigue is added to the equation, not to mention funds for the school. The Charity Trips aspect is based off the burgeoning industry of volunteer tourism. The general understanding of this industry is unclear so before I get into the specifics of Charity Trips, I want to first discuss the industry and how we are looking to amend it into a profitable business endeavor and an enjoyable experience for our target demographics.

It was stated by the Travel Industry Association of America in 2007 that more than 55MM people have participated on some level of volunteer tourism with 100MM more saying they are interested. I am first of all going to cry wolf on these numbers as they are saying that over half of the country has, or wants to, be a potential client of the industry. If I had to take a guess this number is somewhere near half of what they claim, which still represents a 75MM person domestic market with no leader in the industry. There exists a fundamental misunderstanding of volunteer tourism. Currently the companies who are trying to have a go are basically a bunch of hippies who have found a way not to have to return home and probably only make a salary because of the cost of living where they are. There has been a lack of research, a lack of companies, and finally a lack of understanding of how to make the industry go. It is practically impossible to find decent information on this industry with no one doing anything that reflects a sustainable, profitable model. Just cause one is first to the fire does not mean that they have the capacity to put it out.

This is the fastest growing niche in the multi-billion dollar tourism industry just bleeding with opportunity. It will require some pioneering thought as tapping into a passion-industry is quite difficult to monetize. It is worth the efforts to find the recipe because volunteer tourism plays a very large role to both the participants and the recipients. People love doing this, which is why I see it as a high growth niche and the number one reason for participants is without question to do something good. People who like to travel are always looking for something new and exciting to do, tired of the regular trips they can find off the rack.

Currently there is an increased awareness and interest in foreign cultures. If Obama follows the same path as Kennedy, this is the front side of a trend that will expand if history proves an indicator. Anyone can participate in the industry but currently these people are being put to work doing manual labor, which is a difficult concept to sell on any level. When everything is sorted through, the truth of the matter is that there are two distinct types of tourists; volunteer minded and vacation minded. Volunteer tourism needs to better align with the vacation minded tourist as this is where people are willing to spend their hard earned money. Therefore, something must be crafted to bridge this current gap but must result in taking home an experience.

This is an industry that more so than any other, is up for grabs to the company who can do it right and the first one who gets it will be forever associated. Travel bragging is one of the most fundamental things for people who like to go places and try new experiences. People want to be a part of something special and something that has a positive impact on the communities that they visit. Travelers talk, a great deal at that if it is something worth talking about.

Volunteer tourists are seeking something that cannot be received from normal travel and the silver lining of the experience is the positive effect on the travelers themselves. People want to see themselves as growing culturally and want to learn as much as they can about the place they visit. If they do not receive an education around what they traveled across a hemisphere to experience, then they have been failed in not having been provided a special experience. The rewards to the traveler are truly meaningful and assist those learners in how to better integrate themselves to the world as a whole while understanding something that before was never seen firsthand. The experience is one that brings out unique characteristics in motivation and promotes a great deal of self-awareness. In the end, people want to help, gain a better understand of others, and have a special experience.

Non-profit operators have a significant advantage over for-profit operators who are the vast majority representing the industry today. Over a third of the participants who have participated in volunteer tourism have chosen to travel to Central or South America for their experience. A large influence on this figure is the comfort and familiarity with the Spanish language.

In getting into some of my findings one important aspect is to create barriers to entry thus insulating ourselves from the smaller vendors. This is the construction of a school that is happening regardless of any foray into the volunteer tourism industry. A well-conceived school is not something that can be readily thrown up on a whim with a concern for the future well being of the kids. Putting up these barriers will also solidify Hijos first mover advantage that is critical when building a brand and reputation. Vertically integrating the whole process would entitle us to control the experience and promote the safety of our participants to the best of our ability. The quality of food, water, experiences, and guides can never be in question. In the end, satisfaction is the key leading to word of mouth marketing whether in person or through the web as this will be a large factor in driving future traffic. It needs to be designed with no middleman and reservations completed through our website in order to retain the maximum amount of control over the process.

The short-term program for adult participants would be developed a minimum of a year after the school is fully functional. Having a bi-lingual school, it would be good for the kids to be exposed to as many native English speakers as possible. By meeting donors and tourists, I want the kids to be exposed to successful people who can tell them about what it is they do and open many dreams that were unknown before. Forming relationships with donors could provide unique opportunities for the kids in the future and open ongoing sponsorship opportunities.

The days would be broken into two distinct parts with the mornings arranged for classes and volunteering. The classes would consist of teaching the visitors about Argentina, Rosario, Hijos, and poverty. In the afternoons, I would like to see people receive a true Argie tourist experience. Things like going to polo matches, playing golf, fishing (tarpon and dorado), Spanish classes, wine tasting, casinos, factory tours, sailing, cooking classes, shopping excursions, city tours, soccer games, tango classes, or extended volunteer opportunities. Offering a great deal of flexibility to the side trips once people are in Rosario allows them to customize their own enjoyable experience to take home with them. Creating the maximum amount of flexibility in the process allows people to find whatever they are looking for.

At night we would look to have some traditional asados, Argie barbeques, accompanied with great local wine. Throughout the week by experiencing the finest dining in Rosario it would allow a person to sit down with those in their group and make some wonderful friendships. For a one-week trip, we could keep people more than occupied and give them the chance to partake in the volunteer aspect, tourism aspect, understanding of what Hijos is doing, and why Argentina is such a special place. This is a type of trip that no one else would have the capability of offering. Also it is enjoyable to see where the fees from the trips are going with the schools they had a chance to visit, a sort of poetic justice to the tourism industry.

Even though people would be paying to come and visit our operations in Rosario we might as well be paying them for the longer term effects that it would have on their giving patterns. Once the visitors have the chance to get involved with what it is we are doing there, they will not want to be associated with any other charity, at least those that are battling poverty. They will have a new view of the brands that we produce and become a tireless promoter of Hijos. If they choose not, we provided them with dollar for dollar value in the form of a most unique trip to Rosario and Argentina. This type of program would have a positive effect for the city through supporting the local businesses and community of Rosario as a whole.

Before the adult Charity Trips program has the possibility to become a reality we are going to bring in native English teachers through a program very similar to gap year in the UK. Gap year is defined as a period between 3-24 months that an individual takes 'out' of formal education, training, or the workplace where that time services personal independence. In 2004, it was found that between 200,000-250,000 annually participate in some form of gap year aged between 16-24 in the UK alone. Planned and well-structured experiences are greatly beneficial to young people. The trips are often important facilitators in the next step of education or employment with participants gaining a wide range of life skills and other skills relevant to future employment. These skills are often the ones identified by employers as lacking in new recruits and valued by universities. Gap year participation also benefits wider society both in terms of the activities young people undertake and the wider impact of facilitating the integration of young people into society as functioning citizens.

This is a multi-million dollar industry that is growing rapidly and for good reason. There are currently problems with schemes as kids attempt to find reputable programs. As Hijos goes forward beginning to do more and more things, one of our strongest attributes is going to be our integrity and trustworthiness. Traditionally for a gap year type program, students look to align themselves with a program for a time where they can have a culturally rewarding experience. We will become a desirable program offering a safe experience teaching English in our schools but it is more than just that. As the schools are structured to be bi-lingual, an Argie teacher with studies in English will not suffice when it is so easy to bring in native English speakers to the benefit of the kids. Teaching scripted curriculum to kids is really not difficult and the majority of the time would be explaining English words and definitions, sentence structure, and playing.

In researching gap year programs that are based on teaching English in Argentina, I found six. They ranged from three weeks to four months and the average price per week was £350. This seems a bit ridiculous and our program would be significantly cheaper while offering a great deal more in return. It is important to offer Spanish classes so that when they return home a new skill has been at the very least embarked upon during the process. By offering such a program I would hope that we can attract high quality individuals. How I see it, the more quality teachers we have on campus the better education the kids will receive. If we reach the point where there is some financial flexibility in the charity, I will offer these programs as scholarships to good kids with stipends. The more schools that we operate the more opportunity for teaching positions making the experience more enjoyable with a larger base of young, foreign teachers.

Mixing with local staff provides a great opportunity for them to have someone to go out with and experience Rosario with an eye on their well being. There is an active nightlife and our volunteers would be able to collect different experiences based on what they seek. We could even go to the lengths of arranging for the gap year kids to have experiences that they could never find on their own, like meeting people of industry in Rosario who work in their desired professions, attending polo matches, etc. Things that when they go back to university or work the following year, the stories potentially told would make everyone wish that they were fortunate enough to have been a participant with Hijos. Gap year is a wonderful concept and something that enriches a person's life and I am in support of creating opportunities to help.

This program has great importance in regards to the kids as the English speaking students would come as participants for a few months on rotating schedules. By implementing a scripted curriculum there is a short learning curve and in wanting four or so gap year students per class, they can help support and train each other. Residing on site ensures that they are around the kids for extended periods forming influential bonds. This is great in that the kids will learn English quickly and be surrounded by the highest quality young role models we can assemble. The reason people would do this type of trip is to learn and enjoy themselves while doing something good for humanity. We would give a truly unforgettable experience and prove there really is such a thing as a helping high regardless of age or origin.

Detention

The amount of money spent does not reflect the quality of education; it's the thought behind the dollars that creates quality. We can create a dynamic network of schools that offers the finest education available to anyone anywhere. The education begins with a superior curriculum surrounded by an enjoyable overall experience. What makes our curriculum unique is developing it around the concept of having interchangeable pieces. The school will run with rotating two-week programs between Spanish and English. Instead of focusing long periods dedicated to subjects we are going to focus on short bursts of specific topics. All topics will revolve around the real world and are interconnected making all things easier to understand.

A scripted curriculum will allow for consistency to the topics with the shortest amount of prep time for its teachers. After the scripted portions of learning we will break into a question and answer portion that will reinforce the crafted layout yet allow the mind to go where it needs. Scripted curriculum or direct instruction, is considered to be the most effective teaching method for low-income students such as ours in seeking specific achievement levels. Having interchangeable pieces makes it possible to more effectively update portions of the learning and substitute local topics such as history for different geographies. The largest goal behind this approach is that it allows us to standardize the process while making it of the highest quality we are capable. School is mandatory but its not where the vast majority of learning and development will actually take place.

Extra-curricular activities serve multiple purposes allowing for kids to pursue their interests in smaller settings. Learning and development take many different shapes and people are wired to treat formal education different from recreation learning. When activities are chosen for pure enjoyment there is a different group of receptors triggered in the kid that propel the effects of development. Whether it is a coach on the field or someone showing first hand how to make a better art project, everything is more efficient when the kids truly enjoy what it is they are doing. Finding ones passion is something that cannot begin early enough in life and is more valuable than any topic taught. The more we have kids pulling instead of us pushing, the more individual victories will be won.

1) Sports. I grew up an athlete and believe in the effects of learning to play on a team and the intangibles one obtains from the process. Sports are also something that can open doors for students whether they be through the lifelong friendships made or the belief in what one can accomplish when putting efforts towards a larger goal. In challenging oneself to work hard and focus on common objectives, tremendous life skills are established. The first sport that I will facilitate is soccer for obvious reasons and will find a property where we can have a small outdoor playing field. The hours spent outside playing will be vast but so will the smiles and laughter. Maybe someday we will be fortunate enough to have a student we can all go to the stadium and watch play for Newell's.

2) Arts. Expression arts such as painting, sculpture, and drawing are types of programs that will have a large benefit to students. Taking art classes when they are young provides exposure and intrigue. By shifting art to clubs later in school the resources and better instruction can be directed to those who are genuinely interested. This allows students the fullest chance to understand if this is a potential

career and allows Hijos to better manage funds and correlate spending to pull versus push. Film & Photography are great areas to get students involved and can do useful things for the school in the process. Argentina has the leading film industry in South America but before that becomes a reality there are many projects to be done.

3) Languages. The purposes behind learning English and how this will be facilitated has been covered including the rationale for being required by all. Some kids have a knack for learning languages and we will offer them every opportunity to continue. With the world becoming smaller every day, language unveils opportunity. Efforts will include bringing multi-lingual teachers in for our gap-year program as this costs us no more yet facilitates more teaching. As with any of the extra curricular activities when we do not have a suitable teacher on the premises the possibility exists to look into the local community and hire additional staff by the hour. Great employment opportunities follow language skills and direction for further studies.

4) Technology. It is important to cover math and science in class but it is imperative to give kids who have an interest in the subject matter the opportunity to go further. I do not pretend to understand the high tech world but know that people start programming at a very young age and get lost in this world. Bill Gates was 13 when he began programming if that means anything normal. Most people know this

is a great direction but don't know how to get started, as students get a bit older we can bring in people to teach how to begin writing code for programming, gaming, IT, or website development. Allowing for kids to experiment and get started on their own ideas and projects is what will get them excited to the point of considering it as a career with the engineering school in their backyard.

5) Community. Hijos students will be involved in a significant amount of volunteer work for the community. It is important to learn how to give back and I would hope that also this would help them appreciate the opportunities they have been given. Helping to make the community a better place teaches kids something that we can never replicate in a classroom setting. Argentina is not a country where a great deal of charity is undertaken and maybe this can help to set an example but at the very least will be a strong theme internally. Kids who enjoy doing this type of activity can be directed to a number of careers and studies in areas such as social work and public service.

6) Green. Going forward it is important that the next generation has as much knowledge in a green planet as possible. Hijos brands and Hijos schools are prepared to set an example for our students by committing to find responsible green solutions in our operations. Be it converting buildings, using few resources, even looking into how to reuse our scraps from operations is a commitment that is valuable.

Incorporating topics for this category such as marine biology and nature studies will allow the kids to get out of the classrooms and conduct studies in their city about how nature works around them. This is a good introduction to get people interested in health and science professions amongst other green opportunities.

7) Business. Students will have a great many opportunities to be involved with the happenings of Hijos brands and to learn from its operations. Business knowledge cannot start early enough as economics is a fascinating subject and one that is present in every aspect of life with its rules and principles. Creating further learning opportunities in the area of entrepreneurship will imbed the belief that more things can be done at a young age than simply collecting experience. Hijos would love to support students in establishing companies after providing them with the tools and attitude to succeed. This training will lead to future studies in economics, small level ventures, and jobs with Hijos.

8) Hands. Not just students who want to make a career of doing things with their hands should be afforded the opportunity to learn practical knowledge. The more varied the interests of the kids are, the better job we are doing in ushering them down the path of success. Growing up in a boarding school setting the boys would miss out on opportunities to do things such as learn about car engines and carpentry, we are going to help them get their hands dirty.

For the girls, there is a saying in Argentina that when a girl can cook she is ready to get married so we will find some local kitchens and local cooks. An additional area for girls is fashion design. There are many boutiques around the major cities and opportunities to work in the clothing industry. Exposing students to all of these areas would help them understand if they have a talent but more importantly an interest.

9) Politics & World Affairs. These are very important topics that act as a prerequisite for a student who may be interested in the pursuit of law. Offering clubs such as debate not only allows for students to research and learn about new topics, but also allows them to learn how to structure and defend an argument. The chance to delve into the happenings of the world and current affairs is one that students are rarely afforded an adequate opportunity. The world is a fascinating place and one that is comprised of many different leaders and cultures all intertwined. This is important when looking at why the world is where it is today. All history repeats itself and there are no new ideas, just new methods of application.

10) Independence. This is a topic that is not taught as much as it is facilitated. Pick a topic of the previous nine and associated are opportunities to be a part of clubs or conferences around the city or country. We will support and fund students going away to these conferences, gatherings, matches, or whatnot to meet others who have similar interests. As a teenager going

across the country to attend something is a very scary thing but it is something that the students will learn a great deal from. They will also understand that they can accomplish things on their own and begin to wean their dependence off the greater organization. Additionally we do not want every student to have the same experiences and memories.

Los Messitos

The name of the school possesses a tremendous amount of opportunity and strength. There are many ways to look at how to best use the name and I had to go through what it wasn't before I decided upon what it was. The name of a school in a foreign place is not a platform for a donor to attach their name on something when it means nothing to the local community. People from the slums in Argentina have as much interest in foreign donors as they do in sculptors or political figures, but they do love their sports stars. Having a strong name on the school is something that will make the community beyond proud and enhance the depth of how local this school can become from the start. The name on the school will come to attach that person with goodwill in the Rosario area for many years to come and help a lot of people find their futures. The name that has the strongest resonation in the slums of Rosario is the aforementioned

Lionel Messi and I would like to name the school "The Messi School."

The idea for kids from Rosario to attend The Messi School is a quite powerful thing. The name would garner attention and resonate with all types of people. It is possible to brand this kind of school and have familiarity with kids living in not just the Rosario slums, but all Argentine slums. Sports stars mean absolutely everything to the poor and Messi is as big as they come. I could have picked someone lesser known to begin but after looking into it, there was only one person who fit the description and fit it to perfection. The naming would come with no strings attached to donations or appearances as the name was chosen for the kids and no other purpose. If he would like to be involved in any additional capacity, the name on the door would be his.

Messi didn't come from the slums but was not very far removed before moving to Spain. He is a person who overcame challenges when he was young and was fortunate that an organization stepped forward agreeing to pay for his medical treatments. Everything always comes full cycle and where once someone was a recipient of goodwill, there comes an opportunity to return the service to others. I read an interview of his from the other year where he spoke passionately about wanting to help kids leading me to become convinced of the fit. His greatest help would be to continue doing exactly what he is now, being a great athlete and role model for the country.

I understand perfectly well the dynamics of the situation and that it is not ourselves who people line up around the block to catch a glimpse of. There are two realities with the first being our young charity is reaching in regards to early support from an international sports star. The flip side is that we are the only ones who will ever present this opportunity as there is no queue to build schools in Rosario and I do not anticipate this changing. I would much rather recruit someone who offers a potentially special fit and fail than someone who will merely accept or purchase the name. I can only imagine projecting games on the side of the warehouse with kids feeling as if they are watching family play.

Its not traditional in trying to give away the most valuable asset someone building a school has to work with in the name, but the benefits long term make this effort worth it. Even though he is not very well known in the States being a soccer player, he is popular outside and would present the face of a Rosarino. Every school we construct in Argentina thereafter would be a Messi School as one reputable name per country creates the maximum effect. If nothing else, it should make his mother happy.

Snowflake Scissorhands

The creation of a replicable prototype through the Rosario school will allow us to understand how to implement scale. Patience is the greatest virtue behind modeling as everything has its natural order and cannot be forced. Modeling can lead to anything one can imagine and even beyond. Fast food just decades before did not exist with any traction but a prototype was built, or purchased, by Ray Kroc. Today there are McDonalds in 120 countries with over 31,000 locations employing more than 1.5 million people. Say what you want about whether you like the special sauce but those are staggering figures. Size is only a number on a multiplication chart so the focus is not simply in the prototype but how to build the multiplier. Imagine the possibilities if we could build the mystical goose that lays the golden eggs.

How difficult is the idea to model a school for the poor? How many locations around the world have available warehouses and a need for the creation of educational and employment opportunities? A school for kids coming off the streets is not the same as one for kids from typical families and many different things have to be taken into account. There is not an acceptable model of this type of school in existence today to use as a prototype so one must be created from scratch. If the model is not strong then it will crack under the stress of expanding it. The model must be strong where the flex exists in the process and that is in its deliverables meaning where the value is transferred. In McDonalds case, it is in the menu that reinforces the flex of their model. An example being if someone visits a McDonalds in Portland, Paris, Prague, Pusan or Perth a locally tailored yet standardized menu will accompany the familiar environment. In creating a largely scripted education that can flex around local conditions and opportunities, it becomes relevant to each destination within the familiar environment of the larger school.

There are additional points of emphasis when examining the short and long term objectives of replicating schools, decentralization and tangibility. All of the schools must be able to run locally with minimal decisions coming from distance. If we can make it so that the schools have no worries outside of running the best school possible then we will obtain the best results possible. Placing their attention on creating local relationships and delivering a quality local education is all that should be on their radar. The kids who go through the school will become local success stories and local role models to current and future students. Decentralization allows the schools to follow the vision of the larger entity but no school should ever be stripped of its creativity and be expected to do anything special.

Tangibility comes into play in that everything we do has to be measurable. If there is any realistic hope to establishing and operating multiple locations then we must know exactly what it costs to start, operate, and how to evaluate a school. In producing results that can be measured, we will better establish our culture by understanding how to evaluate what it is that we are really accomplishing. Many questions exist that simply cannot be answered today in the required detail but all answers can be found. What does it cost to build a school? To establish a job-training program? To feed a student, or 50? To develop a curriculum? To educate a student? To train a teacher? On top of simply looking at the costs we can compare the different schools to each other in looking at the performance indicators of everything.

Donors are not demanding enough of their charities in what they are producing on a ground level in exchange for their support. By collecting vast sums of information we should be able to communicate at a higher level of understanding with our donors in a shorter period of time. Numbers are boring to most but to me they are imperative when trying to break new ground. By collecting every piece of information possible we will have the ability to make ourselves significantly better by benchmarking the different actions and locations. Better said, we are going to challenge every single aspect of our operation to get better through open competition.

By collecting data we make a new option available to ourselves in the ability to play in real time. Real time communication is of so much value these days with the internet and what people demand regarding the speed of information. Real time is the future for how to best grow a charity. It's always a popularity contest and people vote with their wallets.

Kids who come from the streets have so much potential when backed by a belief in nurture versus nature. There is an indescribable wisdom and hunger associated with those who have not just seen but lived the bottom first hand. When they are provided a direct path to betterment, that opportunity will be realized. To convey that there should be no stigmatism associated with kids who were not raised in traditional circumstances, below are a few names who have gone on to both great and notable accomplishment: Roman Abramovich, Aristotle, Johann Sebastian Bach, Oksana Baiul, Michael Bay, Simon Bolivar, Daniel Boone, James Brown, Truman Capote, Crazy Horse, Daunte Culpepper, James Dean, Edward VI, Alexander Hamilton, John Hancock, Damien Hirst, Faith Hill, Herbert Hoover, Anthony Hopkins, Samuel Houston, Andrew Jackson, Steve Jobs, John Keats, John Lennon, Sarah McLachlan, Thabo Mbecki, Marilyn Monroe, Alonzo Mourning, James Naismith, Jack Nicholson, Edgar Allen Poe, Eleanor Roosenvelt, Babe Ruth, J.R.R. Tolkien, Leo Tolstoy, Mike Tyson, and Malcom X. I hope to add to this list when all is said and done by providing wanted opportunity.

Market Says, Market Does

There exists a vast market as big as people are good that has not yet been properly addressed. There are some groups that do things such as donate profits to charity, selling handicrafts from indigenous populations, imploring a plus one system of one sold to one donated, but these things only hint at the potential market. The real potential to be unlocked is in the job creation required to manufacture the product. Only in controlling both sides of the equation by running our own schools and manufacturing our own product can this vast potential be exercised. Meaning that both goals compliment each other while propelling them simultaneously toward a shared objective. The variable that makes this system credible is that people are good. This is the greatest country in the world as well as the most consumer driven and charitable. A country that supports Horatio Alger stories whether they be for individuals or organizations.

The following are incredibly powerful figures as they are based on human nature. A snapshot of how buying behavior is pro-good and people would like to see more products that follow a proven consumer behavior. A Roper Cause-Related Marketing Trends Report from 1997 out of the UK concluded that 64% of consumers are willing to pay 5% more and 20% are willing to pay 10% more for product with purpose. Additional findings from the Roper study were that 76% of people were likely to switch brands if associated with a good cause, when price and quality are equal. 76% of the respondents also stated that they would change retailers to follow product that supports a good cause, when price and quality are equal. The study concluded that 86% of people have a more positive image of companies they see doing something to make the world a better place. A poll from fourteen years ago in the UK is not an ideal source of data but I would take long odds that in the US today we would find higher percentages in every single category.

My interpretation of these findings is that in competing on level ground with no price injection, we would find both a large and inviting market for our wholly owned and operated charity product. The idea is not to put a plan together for how little we can deliver to people for the money but how much. We can provide everything from including people in building schools in places of need to getting great value for their money through wanted product. With the power today of social networking and the speed of communication, if we are true to what we say the biggest problem we will have going forward will not be demand side. I do not want peoples charity when it comes to their purchases, if they would like to donate we provide an outlet for this but it is not through product. Product is reserved for delivering value. Retailers will work hard to carry our product as it will bring them new customers with no additional advertising dollars spent. An equation where the retailer wins, the supplier wines, the customer wins, the product wins, and the charity wins is what is being shaped.

The setting we are attempting to create is that a customer walks into a store and goes about their normal shopping. If they place the product they have grown accustomed to purchasing side by side to ours, there is no difference in price and quality so why would one not purchase the one that does more? There are many people who are tiring of large corporations and will welcome a new purpose driven organization into the marketplace. We are much closer to people than corporations as we have similar interests, quality at value and helping people (shareholders are not an applicable answer).

The group of customers that we are focused on are the ones who will state clearly and concisely that they could care less who owns the company, they just want the best value. This group is the favorite as we are going to have to work the hardest to make them customers. If we can win this demographic in the marketplace, then we will have access to everyone as we are delivering on a multitude of levels that no other company can compete with. The customers who are interested in supporting and following a charity owned brand will be pleased that we are working hard to deliver our best product at the lowest price instead of taking advantage of their good sentiment. There is a vast difference to an entity that is donating 5-10% of their profits and one who is 100% charity owned and operated. Donating a portion is wonderful but is marketing when for us it is culture.

With our product we are highly conscious of what type of product mix is important, none. The worst thing a company can do in its early years is to have an array of products. Customers typically do not know what they want and the manufacturer should provide their single best product at their single best price to begin. Businessmen are told of the importance of having a varied product line to entice the largest core but this is a fallacy. All messaging can be captured in one product, no wasted motion and it never competes with itself. This also allows us to run a very lean operation eliminating entire departments that will be rewarded with lower prices, better quality, and higher wages. Imagine being a retailer working with an organization when the only number ever discussed is quantity, it simplifies life for all and people appreciate this.

Our model is quite different in that if a person purchases a basic good in a store we may make 35% of that total before tax, but if they donate to our organization we make 100% tax-free for schools. This does not create an unfair advantage in the marketplace as these are two completely separate aspects of existence and better represents what I term as product based marketing. For most companies selling product is the completion of the cycle, for us it is the middle. A traditional company's cycle will encompass one complete circle from start to the decision to remove or reinvest profits. Our cycle is vastly different and better reflects the number nine. The funds in the operating cycle will circle repeatedly as the profits are reinvested in jobs never being removed for profit until it is called upon for education, thus extinguishing that capital by taking it to an altogether different location.

Product based marketing is a way of advertising the charity that creates a significant amount of visibility for both aspects of our operations. Providing yet another example of synergy by pairing charity and commerce. Through product we have the clearest voice possible to a consumer who has already supported the charity making the next transition from consumer to donor all the more realistic. If people like our style of good and believe in education they will expose us to others, this web will grow until we provide a reason for it to cease. Our job is simply to make it as easy as possible to enjoy and share the product while learning about our goal for schools. The best marketing is marketing that literally profits.

Product based marketing can only truly be implemented for a company that aims to exist in perpetuity. We have no exit strategy as the brand is built on service. A for profit company could not purchase the brand and find any goodwill in a brand that is known for creating employment and building schools, nor do we imagine ever selling. All of the concepts behind this idea are exclusively for the long term as this is how to build something healthy. If we put something in motion that is geared for short-term profits then greed will undoubtedly enter the equation taking precedence over balance and stability. If we can always keep the larger purpose in mind, we will find our place in the marketplace with our charity run product.

Cannon Fodder

Bluedo was conceptualized to be the face of Hijos business endeavors. The name Bluedo comes from the Argie word Boludo which is directly translated to mean one with large testicles but not ballsy. It can be used anywhere in a range meaning 'you idiot' to 'hey buddy' depending on the context and is quite possibly the most used word in all of Argentina, it sounds like this anyways. Boludos were 'cannon fodder' or the first troops to be sent into battle and thus the first to be killed. That is probably more on a very common word in Argentina then one ever thought they would know. I latched onto the name after going through some others but this one made anyone who was familiar with the normal usage of Boludo laugh. It acts as an inside joke with the Argies and is as good of a name as any to have, adding a bit of character to the otherwise stale process.

The name is most different but the pattern being followed is anything but. This is our attempt to create a charitable version of a Mickey Mouse type character. The logo that was designed is a blue, fat, happy, smiling cow. In my estimation charity product should be fun and not take itself too seriously. This logo ensures that point but was designed to be quite flexible for going forward. The head and expression of Bluedo are constant but the activity changes depending for what purpose. For example, with the first product being wine it shows Bluedo stomping grapes having purple hooves and legs with juices flowing from the stomping barrel. Being instantly recognizable is most important in attempts to create a visual logo as well as strong color association with the blue from the Argie flag. Coming across as very friendly and approachable is important when looking at how to go forward and keep the maximum number of doors open. Branding behind Bluedo instead of a product, service, or individual will create flexibility and there is no limit or rule in how to apply this. We can brand anything the market will accept behind the smile of our blue cow and the goodwill of his message.

He is a character as much as he is a logo. It's my hope that if we are capable of having some success that future ideas can be positioned around growing Bluedo. After this writing I am going to move into bi-lingual children's books with Bluedo as the star. Other characters that are going to be developed to join him on the farm in teaching kids about giving are Baby Blue (calf), Wings (chicken), Doodle (rooster), Mr. and Mrs. Mud (pigs), Billy (goat), Woolsy (lamb), Woofs (dog), The Polos (horses), and Farmer Mike. We have a chance in writing children's books to not just help people come together with their kids but for ourselves to come together with ours. Starting with the ages of 4-6 the need is great for quality material that teaches more than vocabulary and escapism. Bluedo gives us the recognition that a venture such as this needs in regards to staying power and the visual prowess to captivate young minds. We have to continue to produce until we earn our shot to build schools and use the momentum once created to produce even more.

The finding that led me to children books was from a study conducted by Bank of America on philanthropic habits of high net worth (HNW) individuals. More than 60% of parents are attempting to actively educate their children about philanthropy but there is no good material. 96% of kids learn in HNW families about how to give from their parent's philanthropic example meaning conversations at the dinner table about whatever principles the parents wish to impress upon their kids but we can do one better. Material is how to better bridge not simply the 60% to 96% gap but to strengthen the educational format in the process. HNW families want to aggressively teach giving principles to their kids and if we could choose the most formidable group to form an alliance with, this would be it.

The largest reason people stop giving to organizations, again 60%, is because they no longer feel connected to the organization and 42% of people stopped giving to an organization as a result of being solicited too much. Children's books solve these problems as it is not necessary to press aggressively hard when parents are taking our teachings and making them their own. A market even more relevant for this type of product is not parents but grandparents. It is the type of product that makes for a wonderful gift and is not expensive. It is designed around positive teachings and building bonds amongst those who share the book. A market that is the apex of all markets in one that is shared between kids, parents, and grandparents. Having a variety of offerings over time will tap into the nostalgia created for all three age groups to be embraced warmly. Those exposed to our books would hopefully be willing to learn about our efforts to build schools and become a contributing member of the Hijos family.

If Bluedo gets some traction to young kids it has a chance to develop a totally different line of products than the initial focus. What could follow are things such as toys, games, iphone apps, electronics, clothes, movies, shows, candy, educational material, more books, home décor, collectables, stuffed animals, etc. with each and every one leading to job creation while multiplying the charities efforts to strengthen its brand. We will drive our content around actual efforts to help people placing quality in the forefront and this exposes kids to real world good at a young age. Our bond with customers will be strong as our foundation is not an imaginary world with the underscore of profitability as is commonplace in the children's market today. The Bluedo character has the potential to be something great in itself but will be developed slowly around the larger efforts.

The biggest thing that ties everything from literature, art, characters, stories, products, etc. is it allows us to become closer to customers and donors. We want to be family and remain in the forefront of people's thoughts when they are deciding what charity does a job worthy of their hard earned dollars. We will take advantage of every opportunity possible to communicate with customers and even begin at an age unfathomable to others. If someone trusts our product, the odds are good that they will trust our services.

Vino

I'm not going to bore this writing with the details regarding the history of wine, I'm simply going to discuss why I chose it. In the first venture I have to begin everything from scratch behind an unproven model with the goal of producing clarity. Wine allows us to enter an established market in a limited capacity and grow into ourselves as we prove worthy. Wanting to prove the economics of the idea eliminates the possibility of going directly to manufacturing and in-house job creation. This is for a variety of reasons but the most important is that I am not ready. I must first prove capable to myself by building up a small, private labeled venture before taking quantities of peoples lives in the balance.

Argentina is known for few consumer related products outside the country consisting of Malbec wine, quality beef, and leather goods. Not the lengthiest list ever assembled but one that I've stuck to. Argentina produces a great deal of Malbec wine and it is perceived to have the best value for its price in the marketplace. The wine exists on crowded shelves with many pretty bottles but there is not one label that rises above the rest. This presents a conundrum in that it is promising and intimidating in the same motion. Promising in that there is an incredible amount of potential if we can hit the right tune with the consumer but intimidating in that others have thrown trucks of money at the same goal and missed. We are going to use Bluedo to find our voice in an industry that has low entry barriers and rapid consumption.

So what type of person is hearing the voice we create? Wine drinkers are a higher percentage female than male which is good for us. In the traditional upper income family the man has a larger voice in how the income comes in the door and the woman has a stronger voice in how it heads out the door, including giving. The majority of drinkers are from the Baby Boomer generation and this is the age bracket that has the highest involvement in charitable giving. Wine drinkers are largely college graduates and managers consuming upwards of 88% of all wine, this results in a highly concentrated demographic. The beauty of wine is that it provides the simplest, most direct platform in the marketplace to communicate with people in an unobtrusive manner, the back label. No fancy or expensive ad campaigns pleading with people to listen but fitting into already established lifestyles and characteristics.

In 2008, Argentina exported 52.8 million bottles of wine with approximately half of those going to the US. The other large export markets for Argie wine consist of Canada, UK, and Brazil with a total of 99 countries receiving exported wine. In the US market during economic crises people drink more and cheaper which lines up very well for the market leader in value delivery. For the first 5 months of '09, the US market was represented by a 36% increase in volume and 35% increase in value. This reinforces that the amount of Malbec being consumed is growing at a disproportionate rate when compared to wines from other parts of the world.

The growth of production in the country has been staggering when considering in '02 there were 268 export brands and in '08 there are 972. There are two ways to read into this growth with one being the positive development of the region and an influx of foreign direct investment but the reality is that it has cannibalized individual vineyards ability to separate their message abroad. Using East Asia as an example, the Malbec brand has been deteriorated to death by selling in bulk to the point where the wine will never find a place off the value shelf. This same reputation follows the wine in all markets around the globe making any effort above a modest price point ill conceived.

What we are attempting to do is private label wine from one of the mid-larger sized Argie wine producers. This process is well established and producers are already in possession of all needed bottling and labeling machinery. The wine will be shipped to Miami and the settlement of delivery and payables will be done in the States to great advantage for both parties. Using the producers established import relationship slashes our risk exposure while keeping the process clean to the producer. Once through customs the wine goes to a distributor and then to shelves. Not the most complicated concept and allows us to keep our overhead extremely low. The difficulty lies in reaching shelves when competing with thousands of labels from around the globe. This is why the ability to create a product vacuum becomes so important in maintaining its place on the shelves.

Finding a producer is very feasible and is only reinforced with the current economy. In private labeling, the venture is not restricted to which vineyard the wine is bottled at so long as they have good wine and the capacity to increase volume if need be. Advantages to the producer include profit taking at the earliest stage possible/time value of money earned, reduced risk and borrowing costs, inventory management, cause-based marketing in the States, and doing a good thing for their country. The manufacturers have a good understanding of the fundamentals of our market but very limited in regards to the people here and how to best relate. This is primarily what keeps their wine in the back of the store selling strictly under region.

One of the wine producers I met in Argentina proved to be one of the highest quality individuals I have had the good fortune of meeting in my life. Not in the pages of a book but in reality his employees were treated and respected no different than family. A man who made great effort to support local education and positively impact his local community going beyond anything expected or required. I hope as we progress and find our way that we are fortunate enough to partner with individuals that have their own visions for bettering their local communities.

A distributors dream is to find a brand that has explosive growth potential in a mature industry. Every wine competes on the same basis that their product is superior to competitors at the recommended price. We offer a uniquely different way value is not just delivered but actively participated in. Distributors carry a variety of labels with some selling less than 5k bottles a year and some upwards of 100k. Our approach in creating a voice to our product has the potential to greatly benefit the distributor on a variety of levels but first and foremost is financial. If in the end for whatever reason we cannot find a distributor, we will organize as a wine club with these laws having been relaxed significantly in the last few years.

For all of these reasons along with quite a few others, wine presents both the most effective and most believable path to begin to grow the charity brand. The product made in the Americas to help the Americas will be consumed in the Americas.

The Blue Screw

The wine product is designed to promote itself and to reach new potential donors by a self-inflation process. Working through the in store buying experience there are only two points in play. The first is getting the customers attention to the point of picking up the bottle. The second is actively communicating and enticing purchase when the customer handles the product. Those are the basics of visually branding the product on shelves littered with so many brands but no stars. It is going to be difficult to jump from the shelves but there is a plan. Easy to find, fun to display, uplifting to read, quality to consume, good to give, and drinking to help.

The label will show Bluedo stomping grapes with no text except Malbec and the year of the vintage written on the barrel of the animated scene (by the way, '09 was a great year for Argie grapes as the vintage lags a year from harvest). As I said earlier with Bluedo, product should not be taken too seriously as drinking wine is meant to be an enjoyable process and we aim to comply with that. The plastic around the top of the bottle will be Argie blue to maximize our efforts to visually associate a bottle that can be spotted from distance. The plastic will be over a blue screw top preferring these to traditional cork as it is vastly more convenient, our solo drinkers can thank us later. Asking people to help a charity through drinking is like asking a fat kid to have fun at the buffet or a Japanese girl to have fun at the Hello Kitty store, no problems and enjoyable for everyone.

Communicating through the back label is a quite unobtrusive way to have a chat with someone. The back of most labels tell some story about what the region the wine is from, why it is great, what undertones the wine has, yadda, yadda, yadda, but no one really cares especially at a modest price point. People would much rather be entertained than educated as they have things explained to them all day and drinking is time to relax. It is a platform to briefly let people know whatever we find to be important or interesting. People will find this of great interest as most other bottles all say the same thing and our strategy will elicit long drinking relationships. Being different doesn't mean being loud as much as it means being interesting and understanding our customer's mentality.

I have never known anyone who drinks wine with any regularity and doesn't read the label on the back of the wine bottle. Not to say reading the label in depth as much as glancing over to see if there is anything that strikes a chord. If we are fortunate to get going and have additional runs of product, we will change what is said and have a running dialogue with our customers. Included will be the number of jobs and educations created, our scoreboard. Keeping people updated but never selling as they have already been sold and this does not add to the positive nature of the experience. This is being crafted to become a relaxing product and one to be shared, the bottle will be passed around the table and should elicit good feeling by all. If the process is enjoyable and fulfilling it will develop a core following behind this concept, which is also how a voice is created and how to stay on the shelf.

It is important to point out a central fact about the point of sale. 80% of selling decisions are made in the store with 60% of those people choosing on packaging. There are four main customer profiles that I will describe and then how we relate to each. The first is the inexperienced consumer. Generally university students or the likes, those who drink wine for no reason at all. The second are social consumers who prefer drinking wine in social meetings and are able to identify brands. The third are regular consumers and those are who are used to wine terminology, they think about pairing with dishes and know about brands. The fourth and final are enthusiastic consumers, those who are much more specialized. Who apart from looking for brands, color, and variety are interested in other characteristics such as wine origin.

We relate strongly to the first group through areas of price and labeling with Bluedo, but also behind strong sentiment towards a positive social contribution. Making it the most enjoyable product in its modest price point will relate well to this purchasing group. The second is our core group and along with price, having a recognizable bottle and design will make it easy for continued patronage. This second group is probably the most outgoing drinking group of all and providing them an interesting talking point is valued. The third and fourth groups are the more affluent and foodie crowd. This is the group that the wine being charity owned would resonate most with which can help it overcome being a rung or two below what they have grown accustomed to purchasing. We line up very well here in that our product not only fosters an insider image but also makes for a wonderful gift wine.

The market of gifting wine is not normally an area that is addressed apart from the purchaser as the final consumer. People who gift wine are the best marketers we will ever find and with every bottle having a story to tell, it creates a positive experience for all involved. Everyone gifts wine for some reason or another with strong markets through all seasons and if we can become the brand most recognized with gifting, this is a massive advantage. If any brand of wine can gain traction for this purpose it has to have a good story and elicit a smile upon receipt. This makes it imperative that when someone comes to the wine section in a hurry, they can find us with only a sweeping glance. An additional niche we will sit very well in is the market for charity events and here we are sold in cases not bottles. I could not find any figures on how many bottles are consumed annually at charity functions but there are thousands of events with wine present. There should be no reason not to be received well on the charity circuit being one ourself. We also relate very well to large corporate events by being modestly priced and serving an easily relatable social purpose. Restaurants will have an interest as it is an attractive concept to have helping product on the menu giving their lower price point wines additional character.

In fighting for shelf space we will also perform reverse advertising techniques that are not greatly used but have maximum effectiveness. Putting it out that we would like people to begin writing to their local wine outlets where they shop asking for the Hijos wine to be carried. We will provide Bluedo postcards to supporters to begin writing to their local wine stores and soliciting friends to participate in the same fashion. This is a way to help the charity that requires no money and is the beginning of local grassroots campaigns. Storeowners are trained to listen to customers so we must find a very direct way of communicating while not being invasive, at the very least they will become familiar and aware of the brand. From there it is up to them but the campaign won't cease with one letter or one letter writer, it will be relentless until heard and this is reflected by bottles on their shelves. We don't aim to run like a large corporation but to do our best to become our customer's brand.

It has always been more enjoyable to get turned onto a new product from a friend or through some non-mainstream method. We will not market in the traditional ways for the reason that it doesn't fit our image. The image that we will foster is the perpetual underdog who is going to fight for every inch available. I don't believe that I could bring myself to spend tens of thousands of dollars for traditional advertising when this is money that can be used to change someone's life for the better.

The idea of a product vacuum is setting a series of orchestrated events in motion with the desired end result of product demand or self-inflation. It's a multi-tiered process but one that follows basic logic, good people buying good product.

1) Have great product at value (wine)
2) Cause behind is easily relatable and clear (education for poor)
3) 100% charity owned to prevent skeptics
4) All who help product reach markets profit as normal
5) Advantageous to retailers at point of sale, new customers in the store
6) Visually branded product for easy recognition on shelves
7) People socialize around and discuss larger vision
8) Receive quality word of mouth following behind cause and product
9) Product makes great gift, positive perception
10) Product appeals to, and is affordable to, different classes and cultures
11) Through web able to show tangible results (schools)
12) Some percentage of customers become donors
13) Supplier can handle growth and quantity
14) Brand is versatile and can continue to expand by entering new fields
15) Complete transparency to financials
16) Vacuum in full effect

Skin

Everything discussed up to this point is all leading towards the most influential action, the creation of employment. Outsourcing the wine venture and implementing the first school will establish a brand as well as create the prototype to replicate on the educational side. Having the first school in place will give substance and credibility to the efforts that show exactly what it is we are doing. In constructing the first school, we will pioneer our first job creation program through furniture making. Argentina is a country where the leather hides are more a byproduct of the beef than in any other location meaning there is not and will not be any shortage of the natural resource so long as beef is on the menu. Being able to have factories producing leather goods is not an industry with high start up costs and produces a large amount of zero education, zero experience jobs with strong growth potential.

The leather goods industry in Argentina is structured as having a couple large behind the scenes producers who then stamp the goods with the individual stores label. In asking an owner of one of the stores how it is possible to control the quality of the bags in this scenario, I was told that it is not possible and they are more or less at the mercy of the centralized producer. There are vast amounts of leather goods produced in Argentina as anyone who has visited Buenos Aires can attest to, but the goods have made no headway outside of the country presenting a unique opportunity. Argie leather has quality to match any place in the world with a large percentage of Italian leather goods coming from the exported rawhide. How many cows do you honestly see in Italy? It is the craftsmanship that the country is lacking but this can be taught and even imported. Bringing in a delegation from Italy to teach early craftsmanship will help to establish initial standards and create a strong marketing point. Well worth the cost of a couple plane tickets and a few weeks wages.

In establishing the job training program the first couple of things that we are attempting to find out are basic. Does the person have a strong desire to work and better their standing in life? Does the person have basic sewing skills so that we have an elevated point from where craftsmanship can be taught? And lastly does the person come to work free of alcohol and drugs? This is not a rigorous training program but will teach us whom our future employees will be. There will be no shortage of people from the slums looking for a good job and they absolutely will be good employees. Most people question the work ethic and reliability of these people but I am going to go into the process believing in them as they deserve that much.

Earlier this year I took a bag that I purchased in Argentina around the country in an effort to collect legitimate market information and to better understand how to proceed. I was gone for a month and visited Dallas, Austin, Miami, D.C., NYC, Vegas, San Francisco, and Seattle. I visited with 38 stores including all the who's who; Saks, Neimans, Nordstrom, Barneys, Bloomingdales, Bergdorfs, Stanley Korshack, Prada, Gucci, Escada, Ferragamo, Miu Miu, D&G, Tods, Intermix, Scoop, Zegna, etc. The bag was a beautiful men's weekend bag that I actively use and had purchased for $300 three years prior. There are many ways to track down market information on something but there is no substitute for first hand knowledge as the answers are not always verbal. I took the salespeople as an extension of the customer base and asked quite a few questions in regards to my project gaining tremendous insight not available elsewhere.

It gave me the opportunity coming from a corporate banking background to learn how to go door-to-door which is something never touched on but a vast learning experience. Probably fair to say that many of these salespeople thought I was crazy and quite a few wanted nothing to do with me but I kept on going. Those who weren't too busy which were most, spent a few moments with me to discuss their opinions concerning the bag and the topic of Argie leather. The findings on the bag after throwing out the two highest and lowest price recommendations came in at over $1,000. People like the young classic design of putting the quality of leather forward in a functional no frills manner, an understated quality. Salespeople liked the idea of having a story to sell with the product and the idea of visually branding a quality product altruistically. Argie leather was deemed an opportunity and not a deterrent with the stitching on this bag receiving almost no complaints meaning its more perception than reality. With the bag and leather receiving such positive feedback, I have no questions in regards to the viability of the project though will have nothing to do with a stratospheric price point.

We are not going to have products that compete with our other products. Meaning there will not be multiple designs for similar product type, one product for one purpose. By having a stable group of leather products we do not have to change style on an annual basis but instead would fit into the classic grouping and begin to build our tradition. We do not have the requirements placed upon ourselves in the way that most companies do forcing emphasis on product turn versus the development of relationships. In having a classic look we can allow our sales channels to open at a natural pace as these are looks that will be with us for years. By not placing our name on the outside of our product the emphasis is solely focused on the quality of our goods as this is what will draw attention. Argie blue tags or zipper pulls will become the trademark of the leather goods and over time as the brand establishes traction it will allow for recognition in the streets, the Holy Grail to building a brand.

This was true for things such as Christian Louboutin shoes with their red soles, Prada with their red marking, and Burberry with their plaid. All have created signatures that are equally if not more recognizable than the products themselves. This is what the Argie blue tags will represent over time only coupled with the knowledge that the person sporting it is socially conscious as well as fashionable. It also keeps our costs down in manufacturing as the fewer major steps to the bags we have to do, the fewer costs we will have. The natural leather bag will be accented not only by the blue tag, but the lining sewn to the inside of the product would be blue as well to emphasize the effect. Simplicity will win out over complexity every time when creating something classic.

Keeping the product line clean and modern classic will allow the look to transcend both markets and time. Different markets exist in different fashion times having no relation to real time but product exposure. I want products that will be with someone for decades, aging with them and telling stories of where it has been. Products that will last so they can be given away, passed down, or even donated but the longer they are in circulation the better tale can be told. Looking better with wear and heavy use will only make this bag all the more wanted over time. Having the classic look while being functional will allow the bag to be in places like New York and Miami but also in places that may be cycles behind. All united and linked through the Argie blue tag which means the same thing in all places and helping to build schools will never go out of fashion. Transcending style time and markets gives the bag the potential to be lasting such as a pair of old 501's.

Success or failure will depend on what happens with the brand. Building a leather brand is difficult as is evident from the large number that fail but our message will be clean and precise enough to have staying power. Without that concise message we will get lost in the shuffle make no mistake. The branding is done to promote the blue tag that carries the altruistic association by having something quick and memorable as this is the first step to trigging the message of the larger cause, building schools. This street goes two ways though and there are a great many people who are purely product focused when making purchasing decisions and we want to be able to relate. For them, the blue tag represents quality Argie leather, young classic fashion, and an understated quality.

Momentum must begin somewhere and the key place is the talk in the inner circles. Reaching insiders is reaching trendsetters who will in turn give the product life, real insiders will find you and not vice versa. Once these trendsetters are reached there is an outward expansion amongst trend followers. Traditionally the trendsetters are too small of a group to have visibility. Luckily this outward expansion would be based on the existing brand having been established through wine and taking advantage of a built in market. If we are fortunate to reach the point of producing bags we will transition quickly through trendsetters to trend followers giving the brand both life and a following. Just as people take different ascensions to notoriety, so do brands.

The goal of leather is simple, produce quality at value and keep the prices as low as possible by delivering directly to the end customer. This is why the wine venture is so very important to develop a market of people who are interested in the brand and what it stands for. If people understand that it stands for delivering quality at value, then as we introduce new products we will receive an extended look which is all we can really ask. The lower we can press our prices the more goods we will sell sticking with volume economics. Those economics will allow us to increase levels of production and increase our job count. In becoming a trusted brand we will have a far easier time selling directly from the web eliminating the largest portion of SG&A expenses and deliver low prices.

Coach is the best leather producer around today with public reporting so by better understanding their margins from their last few financials, we can understand how to succeed for the schools. Coach has a gross margin of 75% with SG&A of 40% leaving an operating margin of 35% to quickly summarize an income statement. I do not anticipate we can have a gross margin that high with our economies of scale and the fact that we will be paying higher wages to provide good living wages to our workers. However our SG&A will be nowhere close to 40% either, it will most likely be closer to 10-15% allowing us to use the 35% benchmark as a feasible staging point.

Selling from the website and producing in Rosario makes the leather venture incredibly streamlined. Products need to be thoroughly inspected before being shipped and the cost to ship is $20-60 depending on where in the Americas the order comes from though cheaper within Argentina. Boxes as they go through customs will be opened sporadically but that is customs doing their job and in shipping internationally there is no expedited service. If someone can't employ some patience then walk to the mall as it will take us from order to delivery 4-6 weeks time roughly. The reason for the longer shipping time is that we will work towards producing bags in a just in time (JIT) manufacturing method, after orders are taken they are produced. Beginning under a JIT manufacturing method means that we are being paid before producing the goods keeping our costs down but can be fairly balanced with preproduction in not having an extensive line.

If we look down the road under the pretense that we have success in demand for our leather, this creates a good number of quality warehouse jobs. Warehouse jobs are moving away from the predominately female sewing jobs to male. The warehouses and working with the machinery are more strength related jobs that will be created through programs for ex-convicts. As we look to create positive effects for the slums, the ex-convicts present a unique opportunity. No one will give them employment and it has already been proven in a court of law that they will go beyond the boundaries of normal people. If we can keep this group off the streets then the neighborhoods will become significantly safer. It's my stance that they have paid their debt to society and served their time. In earning a chance at redemption, and it will be earned through good behavior while serving, there is no one who will value the opportunity more.

We are going up against some ruthless people between pimps and drug dealers and it doesn't hurt to have a little muscle on the ground indebted to Hijos. If no one gives these people a second chance at employment they are just going back into their slums as worse criminals then when they left after prison 101. I have jobs that line up with this demographic so why not give them a chance to prove themselves? We will consult with the prisons and organize work release programs to find some people who are good fits for what we are doing. I have no problems with people who were convicted of violent crimes but won't not touch anyone with sexual crimes or crimes against children for obvious reasons.

Today's Tomorrow

If the majority of the poor are looking for and having difficulty finding opportunity, then isn't this the group who we should attempt to create for? Smart kids will land on their feet somewhere but this same thing cannot be said for the poor and uneducated. They will fall and continue to fall until they reach the bottom. We are not going to challenge any accepted fact that is commonplace today, we are going to create mass-employment behind manufacturing because it works and is proven. As Mao Tse-Tung once said, historical experience is written in blood and iron. There is no need to force anyone to do anything because people understand what they need to do and will come running for any and all opportunity which we create. Our goal is not to maximize profitability to no end, it is our goal to be profitable but to invest heavily in our ground level employees and the quality of their life.

If you look back at the overall model it is the intention that the warehouses are to be converted back from schools to manufacturing. The converted schools will have washrooms on location so our employees will be able to take hot showers as being clean provides an added level of wanted dignity. We will provide food in the morning, afternoon, and depending how many shifts we are running later in the evening as well. In addition to feeding our employees we will provide food for them to take back to their homes always giving preference to large families. The greater effect towards the larger picture can be had helping someone with five kids versus one. I will also pay extra if people agree to feed neighbors who may not otherwise eat with an expectation that all employees will exercise this option, however, instead of regulating we will trust them. These things coupled with legal employment and livable wages make for an excellent opportunity to someone from the slum.

We are going to provide a great deal of respect and understanding to people from these locations and do everything in our power to positively effect their life. All that we ask is for our employees to show up on time, be trainable having a willing attitude, also to give us their best effort. If the employees cannot do these things then we will find employees who will. In Argentina, the employment laws are not very favorable to employers but in the first six months of work there is a great deal of flexibility and if we do not have answers by then it is our own fault. I do not wish to get involved inside the employees homes but I do expect that their kids are attending school as there should be no excuse not to. We will provide additional transitional services to help people move out of the slums. Examples of these services are things such as finding a new apartment, school enrollment, bank accounts, anything that may be taken as normal outside of these places but in reality are not.

I would like to have a person in Rosario in charge of local mapping. A rare aspiration to hire a cartographer but I would like to have actual maps of the insides of all the slums creating a war room. This is information that does not exist anywhere and if we want it we are going to have to assemble it ourselves. Having a detailed understanding of the places we are trying to help will allow us to better shape our employment and to clarify how to best assist. Gathering data at the root level of the problems will privy us to all the information needed to solve real problems. Gaining the intimate knowledge of different slums better allows us to track the results of our efforts. Ranging from what is happening with the money that we are pumping into these neighborhoods to how many hands are touching the newly injected capital to how many non-direct jobs are being created inside the slum. The more we know the more we can accomplish and these answers are highly relevant to other places of high-density urban poverty as well as our expansion.

The short-term view regarding employment creation is based on leather goods but there are many connections that can be established from this point. In looking to push costs to the lowest possible level while maintaining the highest quality, we must own our own cattle looking to the mid-term. Rosario is in the province of Santa Fe and in this province are 6.5 million head of cattle making up 20% of the national output. This means that to own our own cattle is a very feasible thought and there is no shortage of experienced local workers or land available to lease for grazing. Owning our own cattle would allow us to purchase calves at the cheapest possible price to raise and slaughter. We would then control the entire process allowing ourselves to give special care to the quality of the hide and the tanning process delivering the highest level of quality in our control. The most important aspect to this idea is that the schools would always have quality cuts of meat, probably lockers full.

Owning cattle is much more than just hides and beef. It is a way for us to hedge our balance sheet by keeping a portion of our capital diversified in readily convertible assets. The Argentine peso is a loose currency but cattle are a global commodity and thus priced on a larger market eliminating a significant amount of potential flux. Also both relevant markets are located in Rosario with futures and commodities so any movements should not surprise us. As we raise our cattle we are growing our capital investment in a variety of ways but most notably keeping our internal costs for beef and hides to a minimum while growing our cash in a hedged position. The expansion of our herd will reflect the growth of our operations as well as being a separate business in itself with ready markets to move everything from livestock to dressed cuts. If this path were pursued we would like to position ourselves to operate our own slaughterhouse to further streamline the process and for the large number of jobs that would be associated.

In looking at the amount of leather we will be requiring from the cattle, the amount of beef that it will produce is disproportionate. An outlet that we could recoup our costs from the cattle and potentially beyond would be in the restaurant industry. Having a lot of quality beef and the means to move that beef will form the needed relationship when coupled with the leather goods company. There is no American BBQ in Argentina but it is a nation that loves meat. They butcher their cattle differently than here and the cuts that we use for BBQ aren't currently employed. If the cattle are our own we can instruct the butcher any way we see fit for our cuts making something difficult to replicate for a potential competitor. What would result is something in between American BBQ and traditional Argie BBQ or asado. The hidden gem in the process is the vast and wanting market available in Argentina for bottled BBQ sauce. If it is done is conjunction with the restaurants it would have a following to begin. An additional asset that would be involved in relation to Hijos restaurants is that we would then operate our own kitchens to provide a central location for the meals required by the schools and factories. The right mix could be found between cattle, leather requirements, and beef consumption levels resulting in little to no waste. The employment numbers of the restaurant would be light when looking at other ventures but the outlet for beef, centralized kitchen, and local visibility is equally as important in this instance.

In reality the first industry that we will enter is furniture making though originally just for the school. One great asset to furniture making is that we would have ready access to leather in Rosario and a known factor in regards to employees. Access to leather scraps can most likely be had at no cost from either our leather operations or those neighboring. This is important because they can be stitched together and do something funky cool with the furniture creating a signature look. Think about a chair with leather on the back and seat with different shapes of brown leather randomly stitched together and fastened on, something West Village though never quite Fifth Avenue. Furniture making can be done made to order allowing ourselves to devise a look in a controlled fashion while maintaining balance with our school requirements. Our quality would increase with every piece completed.

An endeavor branded around the Bluedo character would be the creation of bi-lingual educational material. Similar to the children's books this material is to be developed for the advancement of our own kids but it will also be of great interest to others. There are no start-up costs to this endeavor, as we would use the same staff that has been organized for the development of educational curriculum. What we find in response to the previously released children's books around Bluedo will provide a great many answers as to what type of market would await the material. After working to make its appearance visually appealing, away it goes to the established market for educational material though bi-lingual is not established. It is important that learning a foreign language begins at the earliest stage, even if it is simply an introduction. There is no leader in bi-lingual educational material and not even any visible players. The bi-lingual market is large in the States but even larger outside and can be locally competitive with regional printing. Giving parents the material to teach bi-lingual content without having to speak both languages themselves is the goal.

Some longer-term opportunities become feasible after the leather brand proves the economics of the aforementioned ideas. A logical move for the brand would then be into the clothing industry. With the brand, markets, and delivery system having already been established, the new clothing line would be based on similar concepts to the leather goods. Mainly that there are not a great number of products in the line and the look is clean and simple. Cotton is easily available through parts of Argentina and Mercosur with the line staying in quality fabrics. The Argie blue tag would be carried over from being the leather signature to be incorporated on the clothing and further the visual branding efforts. The clothing industry would be our greatest source of jobs for women living in the slums surpassing leather demand as it deals in higher volume with lower price points. The job count would be easily in the hundreds quickly working towards numbering in the thousands while producing Hijos product in good working conditions with as many hand touches possible. An opportunity even larger is gaining contracts to produce clothing for others. I would imagine us as a prime candidate for government contracts and not just from Argentina. Depending on the success of the Bluedo character, clothes for kids could be an opportunity. If we look to integrate further the possibility would exist to establish our own textile operations and best control quality while lowering costs behind a high job count.

One of the stand-alone companies that there is a need for is quality handmade paper. There is no product in the States that comes close to facilitating this need in my estimation. Handmade paper is very labor intensive which provides the job count to make it attractive but also requires very little investment to get such a company started. An additional related factor is that one of the jobs for those living in the slums is that of a cartonero. This job entails sorting through the trash collecting paper and cardboard to sell to the recyclers and I hope to incorporate this aspect in some regards to our raw material. The handmade paper is a product that is easily packaged, transported, and can be sold online. It can be branded through watermarking and/or packaging. It becomes more attractive with the potential for gift purchases as well as reoccurring use. Furthermore it is a product that has incredible margins.

Construction is probably the highest employer of people from the slums though not with any regularity for the individuals. There is great opportunity to create job-training programs around the needed skills to become carpenters, electricians, plumbers, etc. similar to a trade school. One great need in the Argie market are good remodelers who can guarantee that they will finish the job that they start as there is a problem with contractors walking off jobs stealing payments. Our efforts will create a trusted entity and this trust can be applied with our firm guaranteeing all contracts will be completed as promised. It makes sense to start with remodeling as the jobs are small and very controllable on our part, also paid in advance. Additionally created is a relatively easy structure to facilitate apprenticeships for our students who are not interested in continued education. Other trade schools that may provide value to the local employee base are culinary, beauty, and automotive to name a few.

If we control our own construction labor base then the greatest cost to us at this point would be materials. This is why another company we could look at pursuing would be one that produces cinder block/tile/cement. This is very labor-intensive work but a good job for men from the slums. These materials coupled with labor are the vast majority of what is required in construction hard costs. If we could use product and labor at our cost, we would be constructing at numbers so low it would be unheard of in the market. This would best align with purchasing existing urban structures such as apartments and performing large scale remodels. In these remodels we could further help people transition out of the slums by allowing them to pay some type of subsidized rent in the apartments. Not looking to build five star quality but something that suits our needs, provides good jobs, and delivers on our promise to help people out of the slums.

There are many opportunities of where we can go to create employment in large numbers while still being profitable and benefiting all involved. Through the simple action of looking to pair what the market offers and what we can produce on behalf of the brand it is staggering. There are additional opportunities if the wine is successful moving towards white wine and champagne. If the Bluedo character takes we have the opportunity to produce branded product in many areas related to consumer goods. There is opportunity in Patagonian lamb and wool, Bariloche chocolate, breweries, distilleries, logistics, tourism, private/public partnerships, and this doesn't even begin down the path of job creation in the States. If we have success in dealing with large numbers of employees we will be offered every company of size that is going out of business and the opportunity to buy heavy machinery for pennies on the dollar. There is no end to the potential behind the foundation that we are working to create and the result of every job created translates to low prices for the consumer and building more schools throughout the Americas.

A concept that has been covered indirectly is operating under guerilla economics. One voice to multiple industries and through decentralized operations they will grow at different speeds in different markets. Operating in small groups allows us to move rapidly and quietly into vulnerable positions of our competitors. It is the idea of hunting in small packs versus being hunted as happens with the oversized. The rear of the larger competitors is where our market will develop from yet we have no visible rear. From the start a premium is placed on imaginative leadership, distraction, surprise, and mobility allowing us to pick the most favorable ventures and investments to pursue as resources will never be unlimited. If we place all our resources and hopes in one thing that does not prevail all is dead. If we can spread our resources across a few industries we could move employees to where expansion is needed building something fast and responsive with a taste for blood.

The journey is not short term and we will see good cycles and bad, but our commitment will always be to our employees before profits. It is not the end of the world to have a no-growth,

no-profit year if that means keeping all the jobs
we have worked hard to create.

The Looking Glass

A quarrel had arisen between the Horse
and the Stag, so the Horse came to the Hunter to
take his revenge on the Stag. The Hunter agreed
but said: "If you desire to conquer the Stag, you
must permit me to put this piece of iron between
your jaws, so that I may guide you with these
reins, and allow this saddle to be placed upon
your back so that I may keep steady as we follow
the enemy." The Horse agreed to the conditions,
and the Hunter soon saddled and bridled him.
Then with the aid of the Hunter the Horse soon
overcame the Stag, and said to the Hunter: "Now,
get off, and remove these things from my mouth
and back."

"Not so fast, friend," said the Hunter. "I
have now got you under bit and spur, and prefer
to keep you as you are at present."

In working in different countries and
locations we are going to encounter every type of
government and personality. I will work with
any government that is in office and I am sure
they will support our efforts as we are seeking
nothing in return. There is the reality local
officials will want to use Hijos as a vehicle in
regards to elections and our relationships in the
slums. I will not publically support or voice
opposition to any candidate under any condition

117

taking a long-term Swiss role. Our model calls for funding to be derived thousands of miles away meaning we are not dependent upon local conditions allowing us to escape the potential bit and reins to the best of our ability. If elected officials would like to solicit our opinions or information we have gathered, our doors are always open to help. This goes for local churches or charities as well, if we can assist others who have the same goal of helping it is no problem as we are all on the same team. There is no glory in isolating success at the expense of real people as the information gathered has the most power when shared.

In offering employment to the poor and returning the profits to the local communities we are in some aspect pure. We are not victim to arguments of greed and management exploiting local workers. We cross all the stated boundaries between traditional Republican (red) and Democratic (blue) lines. This is an extreme red charity in that it is not built to just be sustainable but high growth and to support its growth through self-created efficiencies. This is also a far blue charity in that we are going to the poorest communities in the Americas to create schools and jobs asking nothing in return. Built to align with the interests and opinions of the wealthiest as well as to align with the interests and opinions of those with nothing. We relate to everyone in the spectrum. We are everything and we are nothing.

A choice was made not to run this as a for profit company so that the results can best be given to others in a perpetual fashion. Could there be a better life than one where you come into the world with nothing, go out with nothing, and create everything in the process? Most choose to amass their wealth and at the very end give it to worthy causes. I don't see the pleasure in collecting as much as possible only to leave it as a line item on a will. Wouldn't people rather see what their hard earned money could accomplish when mixed with something a bit higher octane? The true bottleneck to the system is bringing in quality to run the charities as most with a focus on business and entrepreneurship do not enter the non-profit world. Capitalism is the greatest system in the world but it only works when money circulates. Social progress works in tandem with capitalism if it is structured to do so but if not, it is an insurmountable task to blend the ideals of each.

Each aspect will have its own method of how to listen to the groupings of students, workers, and community. The student's feedback will come from the students themselves and their student council. Disciplinary methods will be handled similar to a kangaroo court. These students are going to be given more responsibility than most and at a young age but the school must be theirs. Employees will rotate and volunteers will come and go but the students are the constant. For the first time they will have something real and theirs. Schooling at a young age must be fun for the students, if we hear feedback that it is nothing but work then we are failing. Some of this is experimental management regarding schools and some will say they are too young for responsibility but they were never handled with kid gloves. Kids from the streets have incredibly high levels of wit as they have never even been exposed to the easy way.

I do not anticipate having a need for an outside union but we will structure a very strong internal one for the employees. It is from this group that we will learn how to better assist our workers with their lives. Obviously wages are a major concern but if you give more responsibility to the workers they will do a better job than if simply told what to do. Shared responsibility is the quickest way towards efficiency. They will know what production is required of them and I would rather have a factory full of teammates than two competing sides. Workers are not accustomed to companies who return their profits into the community with owners not taking their profits for personal advancement. Even the lowliest worker can walk around town with their head held high knowing that they are contributing to a better community. The factories will have a strong voice in how to get better and that voice will be listened to and valued.

The last area we are looking for feedback is from the customers and donors. We want to know from people how we can better deliver value. Our entire business operation consists of listening to customers, that doesn't mean catering to every word but typically the answers are somewhere between what is said and what is implied. Instead of constantly soliciting donors to give more, I want to know what it is they want in exchange for their giving. Nothing is free in the world and neither is people's charity. Maybe it is wine, art, trips, trust, or transparency but there is always something. In regards to being located in Miami we are in the center of the Latin community and we will hear feedback relayed from our locations.

The conclusion is simple as there is not a company or charity being created but a family of opposites. A family that includes people from the lowest walks of life, kids without homes in third world slums; to people from the highest walks of life, donors from the States who were born into fabulous wealth. Our family will include governments from the left to the right and every ideal under the sun. The most famous of athletes to the most forgettable of convicts will be considered family. It is a family that will have the face of a cartoon character and costs nothing to be a member of, just a belief in that to make a difference action must be taken. There is no limitation to the size or the geography of the family being assembled. To believe in something doesn't require a passport or pedigree, just the support of a vision. It does not matter to this family what you are but who you are.

Bowl Game

Our donor relations are something that cannot have a large enough emphasis placed upon them. It is one of the fun areas in which we can craft a method that is not being practiced making it uniquely our own. Just having a large party where people get dressed up to attend and donate is quite one sided in the charities favor. More can be done to better appreciate the donors who will make our efforts going forward possible. In how to formulate a strategy towards donor relations there are two positions that must be considered, the constant over the course of the year and the one time event. The conveyance of information is our most powerful tool and must be utilized to maximize the charities efforts to create a strong following. Donors cannot be imagined as appearing out of thin air and must be cultivated.

The constant to keep people returning to our site is an online magazine. By circulating content we'll provide a reason for people to regularly visit our site and build a content driven relationship. Setting up an online magazine does not require more than a person or two to begin and would be comprised of interviews, donor profiles, fundraising news, operating news, announcements, employee profiles and stories, new projects, brand news, sales updates, new markets, but most importantly stories about our schools and what we are getting done. The magazine opens an audience that is as large as the internet is wide. Ensuring that we do not disappear into a local bubble when it comes to keeping a consistent flow of information to those interested regardless of geographic location.

Donors need to be better informed about their charities and what exactly they are doing. An online magazine is a tool to bridge this shortfall while doing so in a voice that emphasizes the strengths of our positive efforts. I want people to be proud of what we are doing with their hard earned money and look forward on a monthly or quarterly basis to when the new edition is released. Keeping the line of communication open in a much more enjoyable way than a mailing that comes with a short thank you and a return envelope looking for an additional contribution.

The one time event begins local and ends global. There is everywhere else and then there is the State of Miami. Just as the efforts of our social actions are location based, so are our fundraising efforts with Miami acting as the anchor. The State of Miami encompasses Miami, Miami Beach, Aventura, Coral Gables, Ft. Lauderdale, Boca Raton, and Greater Palm Beach. Maybe Manhattan comprises a higher concentration of wealth but The State of Miami is a world of its own. There is no secret formula to how to get a charity up and off the ground than beating the pavement and working hard. I am going to go around South Florida and speak anywhere they will have me about this charity in an attempt to find quality people and go from there. The rest of the country will be what it is going forward but if we are not capable of creating traction in our back yard then how is it believable to imagine doing so anywhere else? I arrived in South Florida with the intention of matching opportunity to location and will work tirelessly to do so.

For our main event I am going to create a bi-lingual documentary film on an annual basis. Between the people, kids, multinational donors, and myself one language will not be adequate. As we film two languages will be present and rotating subtitling between the languages will allow the two worlds to coexist, very clean and easy. A documentary does not require a great deal of funding to put together and will be a great deal of fun to watch. Much of the filming will be done around our schools and when cameras are around, it's a given that kids are going to show off resulting in some humorous scenes. Making it easy for people to see exactly what it is that we do on a ground level is of great interest. Taking them into the slums, schools, and factories will show how we are literally changing lives through providing opportunity. This will resonate strongly when viewed in a theatre setting and even more so when surrounded by people whom share the same belief. It will be the centerpiece of an event but grows exponentially after the first showing in that it can be redistributed on a larger scale.

The Miami event will be at the Gusman Theatre with invitations sent to our favorite donors creating a version of our charities Oscars. The Blue Carpet will be rolled out in front of Miami's most famous theatre that seats up to 1,500 people creating a unique atmosphere that would have no peer. A movie allows us to market the event as something exclusive but also something that we can repeat on an annual basis creating a regular following. If it finds traction we will have not just our State of Miami donors present but people coming in from all over the States and even internationally to show their support and meet others from the Hijos family. It is our goal to create an event for the Americas that will showcase its greatest humanitarians.

Before the event we will have our annual shareholders meeting. Donors are not shareholders but should be shown the same respect for their hard earned dollars. Transparency is key to any company and any charity for that matter. This meeting would announce our direction and goals for the upcoming year while celebrating those met in the previous. If we want our donors to be family they must be given a chance to be heard and this meeting provides a serious stage where this can be accomplished. Opening the stage for donors to question management and why a particular direction has been taken or why costs are what they are in a particular area. One person must always be held accountable for the organization and this is a way for myself to forfeit any type of safety net.

The accompanying annual report will be sent out to each and every donor along with a copy of the documentary film. Every one who donates from whatever corner of the world should receive the efforts of our transparency. People who donate fifty dollars or fifty thousand dollars deserve the same quality of information. The fifty dollar donation may have created greater hardship to the donor and if one believes that people with an income under $40k donate a higher percentage of their income than those with an income over $100k, it may very well be true. What is important is that all our information is open to everyone and we are responsible for the entirety of our actions and their recourse, positive or negative.

Our relations are going to be developed both locally and globally through different measures. Some like the glitz and glamour of a party while some like to understand what is happening with their giving in the privacy of their home. No person enjoys being the recipient of a hard sell and the conveyance of relevant information should be the cornerstone of any quality sales or appreciative effort. We are going to offer the most respect to the giving process as we can fathom and at all times remain open to any race, creed, color, national origin, sex, sexuality, political affiliation, or belief.

Infinity Edge

The goal of running branded ventures is to allow a 100% flow through of peoples donations to ground level distribution. It will obviously take some time to build but the premise is achievable. The money made by the companies goes towards picking up the tab for not just its overhead but also the overhead and operations of the charity. The donor money follows a good lead block of the company allowing the entirety of one's donation to go exactly where it was intended, to the cause. There are no dividends or shareholders to pay so if we can build our companies to become profitable we are going to be parlaying the profits to no end. The pleasure of traditional giving extinguishes itself relatively quickly while we have constructed a better drug.

The start-ups will be funded through funds raised for the establishment of an endowment. Many charities have endowments that seek a return on their capital and we will seek ours while creating jobs along with a brand in the process. Interest will be paid equivalent to A-rated bonds back to the endowment to use this interest in the schools operations. Our start-ups will be funded in their entirety through this manner which will ensure that we have no exposure to credit or external investors in the early stages. We reserve the position to take on some leverage at a later date once our sales growth better mirrors our employment growth but we will not build a paper dragon. I am allergic to credit and believe in a pay for play attitude so that we are never playing with more than we can afford to lose. All donations to the charity will be through checks or wires meaning credit card payments will not be accepted. If someone cannot afford to donate from what they have then we are not going to encourage one to keep up with the Joneses.

The better the performance of the company means better visibility for the charity and they will rise or fall together, bound to each others success or failure. It does not cost a fortune to build schools from warehouses and these costs are both fixed and frontloaded. The required costs to follow the full property conversion will have been previously pioneered by Hijos and made manageable through working pipelines. The operating costs of the schools are quite minimal when looking at the great return for the kids and further subsidized by the Charity Trips programs and interest earned by the endowment. This will permit donor's money to venture beyond the schools operations to push forward in a financially responsible manner to establish additional schools. The combination of the maximum flow through of donations and earned income when coupled with an objective that is not cost intensive will make a tremendous impact. Typically when one hears of a program with 100% of donations making it to the cause there are some deep pockets behind the scenes, this is not our case as we can offer wit and wisdom but no wallet.

Churchill said that it is a mistake to look any farther than one link of the chain of destiny at a time as it cannot be handled. I have made my best effort to discuss not only the application of the upper diamond and its relevance but how this creates the necessary transition to the lower diamond. The double diamond is merely an aid to help ones mind follow the logic of the demanding path towards the creation of large-scale opportunity for the poor. There is no original thought in this writing as I looked to my idols of Henry Ford and Marcus Aurelius in many instances but there are original combinations. Great thoughts are meant to be used again and shared with new generations, which in turn reinforces their quality and perpetuity. By reading and understanding these thinkers it becomes possible to better pair modern day benefits with the application of their practices. Instead of thinking exclusively about the end game, the emphasis is placed on how to use the process in order to help as many people as possible along the way as this ideal has been misplaced over the years.

The most important aspect of the thinking in this writing is that it all works within the framework of today's reality. The beginning of any great effort has to be present in time and have the capability of assimilating into the framework of the available system or systems. It is not realistic to draft ideas from perfect settings and make noise about how things should be, it must be how it is or we are no different than the many who have spilled ink before. Ideas are pretty but the application is how quality separates and where the true beauty resides. People must be able to see a larger perspective in what they are working towards putting aside the need for instant gratification as it rings hollow.

The objectives of what we are hoping to accomplish reside in half-decade blocks. In the first block the goal is to have the Rosario school established and the branded wine company developed. An understanding forged of how to bring a school out of the ground and how to fill it with the kids it is designed to help. Having a bi-lingual curriculum ready for the kids up to age ten and a working pipeline bringing in Charity Trip participants. The wine venture should be profitable and expanding its geographic market with a working knowledge of how to transition customers to donors. In having a working school we will also be able to make a documentary film and online magazine beginning to change how a charity can communicate as well as entertain its donors. This block encompasses the first diamond.

In two blocks time, the goal is to have the leather company launched, cattle operations, and two schools established in Argentina as well as entering a new country for our third. Rosario will become the headquarters for the schools located in Argentina and the decentralized oversight process will be underway. The model will then go outside of Argentina for the first time to open a new school to become the headquarters of a new country. The initial location in a country will be the manufacturing hub for that particular country thus our national headquarters. In having the leather company running we will have the understanding of how to implement our job training programs and create jobs for the poor. If we can hit the goals laid out, expansion will happen quite fast thereafter but the beginning cannot be rushed as it must be correct or else we are building on mud. The second block completes the working double diamond model.

There are only 9 areas in which we will evaluate our progress.

1) Jobs created,
2) Schools built/students,
3) Quality of education,
4) Head of cattle,
5) Cash flow of companies,
6) Value of Hijos brand,
7) Number of online followers,
8) Amount of data collected,
9) Attendees for annual event.

One America

From the tip of Canada to tail of Argentina is one large connected body of America. South of the States consists of more than 570 million residents making up 8.5% of the world's population. Yet America must become reacquainted with America. A desire to involve itself in the process of taking people that are perceived as trash and turning them into treasure. Dealing a new hand of life to those who have nothing but the ability to pray for a miracle. There are so many voices that the sound is deafening.

To one day walk into a school and be surrounded by hundreds of kids who until recently were eating out of dumpsters is accomplishment to the highest degree. To one day staff a factory with hundreds of people who until then had no place to go to put food on their family's table. Take these examples and replicate them to service a bottomless demand and those prayers are being answered. With more than 50 cities having in excess of one million residents in the lesser-developed America, it only places more of an emphasis on finding real solutions to high-density urban poverty. Progress must begin where it is most difficult creating impactful results for the benefit of society as a whole.

Progress will begin with the education of the poor. Taking kids off the streets who without any help will undoubtedly become the future of drugs and prostitution in their neighborhoods. In not accepting what is considered a suitable education for the poor, we will create something that delivers actual advantages beginning with the English language. Making the kid's futures more relevant by incorporating the real world into the most effective teaching methods known today. Giving them the tools to leave the world of dire poverty and enter the functioning city wherever this may be to aptly succeed. Surrounding the kids with people who care about them and want to help them become quality people for their journey through life. Our students are our progress.

Progress will begin with not accepting conventional wisdom for how a business should operate. Achieving a positive impact on all who are involved in the journey, not just the destination. Changing the script in that factories are meant to provide for the people instead of people for the factories while still following the guidelines of capitalism. Creating the greatest and most beautiful product of all, mass employment, as through this we will take the utmost pride. Going into neighborhoods with astronomical unemployment rates and providing opportunity for those who wish for a better life torpedoing long-standing problems. Companies founded and branded around a cartoon character that represents something much more than a business but a family. Aiding people all the way out of the slums by providing livable wages and a working support network. Our employees are our progress.

Progress will begin with giving customers something more than they have grown accustomed to. Creating a greater story than anything that has come before, a spectacle of product with tangible results at the end of the performance. Listening to the customers to ensure that our products are not simply created as a hollow means to employment, but to answer the voice of what is lacking in the marketplace, both altruistically and commercially. Allowing customers to play a role in real progress through an act they were already planning on performing. Not a bond of company and customer but something stronger, more lasting and indescribable. Our customers are our progress.

Progress will begin with better serving donors. People who will hold us accountable to our commitment for not just smarter solutions, but our desire to treat them with no less respect than shareholders of a publically traded company. Exercising the unlocked potential of an endowment to not only return a percentage but also to create both a unifying voice and large-scale employment. Fashioning an online magazine to keep contact throughout the year with a global base and a destination style event that features our annual bi-lingual documentary. Maximizing the amount of donor's money that flows from A to B in a sustainable fashion enlarging the smiles on both sides. Making it easier and more appealing for those interested in visiting the actual operations to do so while enhancing themselves in the process. Our donors are our progress.

As Woody Allen once said, ninety percent of life is just showing up and we are here. This writing wasn't done to be perfect, it was done to be me. To show that adversity is the first step to truth, to inspire others with great hope, great courage, and going forward, great achievement. By boldly sharing an idea of how to change what help can be, we thus craft the stage to contribute to the advancement of the Americas. Important is not where we come from but where we are going, to mass-produce miracles.

I am William Wallace.

"Unconquerable"

A short poem by English poet William Ernest Henley that was first published in 1888. It was written in a hospital bed bringing this writing full circle back to nowhere from everywhere.

Out of the night that cover me,
Black as the pit from pole to pole,
I thank whatever gods may be
For my unconquerable soul.

In the fell clutch of circumstance
I have not winced nor cried aloud.
Under the bludgeoning of chance
My head is bloodied, but unbowed.

Beyond this place of wrath and tears
Looms but the Horror of the shade,
And yet the menace of the years
Finds and shall find me unafraid.

It matters not how strait the gate,
How charged with punishments the scroll,
I am the master of my fate:
I am the captain of my soul.

To contact me or learn more:

Mike Stewart
mikeinargentina@gmail.com

www.hijosonline.org

Hijos de Argentina
P.O. Box 12231
Miami, FL 33101

EIN# 75-3262225

Made in the USA
Charleston, SC
24 February 2010